shaping
business leaders

shaping
business leaders

WHAT B-SCHOOLS DON'T DO

Asha Bhandarker

Research Group

R Ravi Kumar
SG Bhargava
Pankaj Kumar

Response
Business books from SAGE
Los Angeles ■ London ■ New Delhi ■ Singapore
www.sagepublications.com

First published in 2008 by

 Response Books
Business books from SAGE
B1/I-1 Mohan Cooperative Industrial Area
Mathura Road, New Delhi 110044, India

SAGE Publications Inc
2455 Teller Road
Thousand Oaks, California 91320, USA

SAGE Publications Ltd
1 Oliver's Yard, 55 City Road
London EC1Y 1SP, United Kingdom

SAGE Publications Asia-Pacific Pte Ltd
33 Pekin Street
#02-01 Far East Square
Singapore 048763

Published by Vivek Mehra for SAGE Publications India Pvt Ltd, typeset in 11/14pt Sanskrit-Garamond by Star Compugraphics Private Limited, Delhi and printed at Chaman Enterprises, New Delhi.

Library of Congress Cataloging-in-Publication Data

Bhandarker, Asha.
  Shaping business leaders: what B-schools don't do/Asha Bhandarker.
    p. cm.
  Includes bibliographical references and index.
  1. Business schools.   2. Executives—Training of—India.   I. Title.

HF1171.I4B43   658.4'092—dc22   2008   2008023506

ISBN: 978-81-7829-845-0 (PB)

The SAGE Team: Sugata Ghosh, Koel Mishra, Gautam Dubey and Trinankur Banerjee

Dedicated to

Management Guru and Philosopher
Dr P. SINGH
Prof. of Eminence-MDI-Gurgaon, India

Contents

Contents

List of Tables

List of Abbreviations

AICTE	All India Council for Technical Education
M	Mean Value
SD	Standard Deviation
BRIC	Brazil, Russia, India and China
B-School	Business School
Rho	Rank order coefficient of correlation
N	Number of persons in the sample
Sig.	Significant
ESA	Emotional Self Awareness
EAO	Emotional Awareness of Others
INT	Intentionality
RESI	Resilience
PO	Positive Outlook
COMP	Compassion
EMEXP	Emotional Expression
IPC	Interpersonal Connection
CONSDIS	Constructive Discontent
TR	Trust Radius
CR	Creativity
IN	Intuition
TIA	Tolerance–Intolerance of Ambiguity

FLEX	Flexibility
Bajaj	Jamnalal Bajaj Institute of Management Studies
IIMA	Indian Institute of Management Ahmedabad
IIMB	Indian Institute of Management Bangalore
IIMC	Indian Institute of Management Calcutta
IIML	Indian Institute of Management Lucknow
MDI	Management Development Institute
S.P. Jain	S.P. Jain Institute of Management & Research Mumbai
TIA	Tolerance–Intolerance of Ambiguity
TR	Trust Radius
XIMB	Xavier Institute of Management Bhubhaneshwar
XLRI	Xavier Labour Relations Institute

Foreword

There is a crisis of leadership in the contemporary business world. Today it is difficult to find the right kind of business leaders who are not only sensitive to the broader sociocultural and environmental challenges, but also enthuse and carry people towards the larger goal. While predicting the future of economies and nations, the *Goldman Sachs report* clearly indicated that the future belongs to Brazil, Russia, India, and China (BRIC countries), who are poised to become the major drivers for the globe. The paucity of leaders becomes critical when viewed in the framework of the huge challenges and available opportunities for India in today's world. To realise the Goldman Sachs prediction, India needs a huge supply of leaders who (among other things) can manage complexity, manage diversity, influence others and above all, manage themselves and others.

Management schools worldwide have been criticised by both academia and corporate executives. Scholars like Mintzberg and Bennis have been sceptical about the role of B-Schools in grooming managers and leaders. I have also heard similar comments and opinions in India about the role of B-Schools, both from the corporate world as well as from academicians.

In this perspective, therefore, this book is a thought-provoking contribution to our understanding of the impact of management education in grooming leaders in India's top B-Schools. On the one hand it throws up issues of the kind of leaders the corporate world would need and on the other, it throws light on the kind of leaders B-Schools are grooming. The author has highlighted four broad leadership capabilities—managing self, influencing others, managing complexity, and managing diversity—important for leading in a dynamic, discontinuous, and global world. By studying the expectations of key stakeholders—corporate executives from management graduates, Dr Asha Bhandarker has mapped out the desired direction in which B-Schools need to move to be relevant to the corporate world.

This book is an excellent contribution to the scarce research on Business Education in India. The book is based on rigorous and painstaking work of the research group. It uses a longitudinal approach to data collection and has a large sample size which lends credibility to the findings.

The book contextualizes the current status of business education in India by comparing the same with some of the leading American B-Schools such as Kellogg, Ross School of Business, Wharton, Darden, and Weather-head School of Management.

The book is rich with insights which can help management schools to re-examine and re-orient their philosophy of education, pedagogy, as well as their curricula. It will also help potential management graduates understand corporate expectations and enable them to identify areas for self development should they choose to get into a corporate career. The findings of this research will help the corporate world to identify the gap between their expectations and reality and enable them to develop more sharply focussed induction and training programs.

Reading this book has made me reflect on the state of management education in India. If leaders are not being groomed in India's top schools—the role models—it is a matter of great concern as to what might be happening in the other schools across the country. I am pondering on the role which AICTE—All India Council for Technical Education—can play in promoting high quality education which could be useful and relevant for the corporate world.

I am very happy to note that this book is an outcome of the research work funded by the AICTE. The objective of the AICTE—to enhance educational quality and standards—is met by such a work. The book is bound to have a far-reaching impact on B-School education in India especially at a time when the country is in the process of revamping management education.

I congratulate Dr Asha Bhandarker and the research group comprising Professor R Ravi Kumar, Dr S G Bhargava, and Dr Pankaj Kumar for undertaking such a seminal research work.

June 2008

Dr R.A. Yadav
Chairman
All India Council for Technical Education,
New Delhi, India.

Blueprint

I distinctly remember my flight to Bombay in November 2000. I had the privilege of flying with a distinguished business icon of this country, very well respected and known for his capability to build a great business empire. While discussing many general issues, he sprang a question, 'What do you do?' I replied, 'I am a Professor in a leading management school—MDI—and we groom future business leaders'. He tried to control his surprise and said sardonically,

> Oh! This is interesting! Do business schools really groom leaders? My experience with scores of MBAs from the top Indian schools tells me that business schools tend to produce job-hoppers, careerists, and climbers. Their life ambition seems to be reaching high positions rather than make contributions to nation building. It's a pity because, these are some of the brightest minds this country produces.

I was stunned by the intensity of his antipathy towards B-School graduates.

He continued his reflections and raised a second question,

Tell me, what percentage of MBAs have actually built business houses as compared to others? How many have been of the stature of a Bill Gates, Steve Jobs, Sam Walton, Michael Dell, Narayana Murthy, Aditya Birla, Azim Premji, Sunil Mittal, LN Mittal, or Ratan Tata?

He further said, 'I don't wish to offend you or B-Schools, but the reality is that B-Schools world-wide haven't succeeded in grooming many leaders.'

This episode struck a raw nerve. I was agitated about this matter and discussed it with some leading names in the field of Management. People said that rather than being agitated, it would be better to examine and validate the opinion. I chanced upon a piece of work on the role of education by UNESCO, which stated that the aim of education is to enable people in:

- Learning to learn,
- Learning to do, and
- Learning to be.

These high ideals together facilitate the holistic development and evolution of a person making them truly self actualizing and evolving. Both these events further reinforced my desire to take up the study of the impact of B-School education on grooming future leaders.

During my Fulbright visiting professorship (2004–2005) at the Darden School of Business, University of Virginia—one of the top-ranking American B-Schools—I also took the opportunity to visit Kellogg School of Management (North Western University), Ross School of Business (Michigan-Ann Arbor), Weatherhead School of Management (Case Western), and Johnson School of Management (Cornell University), to study these business schools and compare Indian schools with them.

This book is an outcome of my research in India as well the anthropological experiences and interactions in the American B-Schools. This book is organized in four chapters:

- Chapter 1 deals with the introductory frameworks of this study, encompassing literature survey and methodological schema,
- Chapter 2 examines the profiles of B-School graduates in the eyes of the corporate executives and alumni,
- Chapter 3 presents the profiles of B-School graduates at entry and exit levels and also assesses B-School impact on the graduating students, and
- Chapter 4 highlights the salient findings and maps out future direction for B-School education.

I would like to express my gratitude to AICTE for their generous funding of this work. Distinguished Indian management thinkers—Dr Pritam Singh, Prof of Eminence, MDI; Late Dr Dharni P Sinha; Dr R A Yadav, Vice Chairman AICTE; Dr Devi Singh, former Director of MDI and presently Director IIM-Lucknow; Dr T N Kapoor, former VC Punjab University, Chandigarh; Dr B R Sharma, former Director Shri Ram Centre for Industrial Relations; Dr B S Sharma, former Dean FMS, Delhi University and currently Dean Kota University; Dr S P Parasher, Director IIM-Indore; have helped me in developing a perspective on management education in India and I would like to thank them for this. I would like to say thank you to T L Sankar, IAS, my first boss at IPE, Hyderabad, who always reminded me that the role of a scholar is to research and publish, thereby using the power of knowledge to improve society.

I would like to acknowledge the following professors for generously sharing their views and opinions on management education, thereby enriching my perspective—Deepak Jain (Kellogg School), Noel Tichy, Kim Cameron and Wayne Brockbank (Ross School of Business, Michigan), Richard Boyatzis, David Cooperrider and Suresh Srivastava (Weatherhead School), Roger Stough (School of Public Policy, George

Mason University), and Michael Useem (Wharton), among others.

I would like to express my heartfelt appreciation to Professor Ravi Kumar (IIMB), Professor S G Bhargava (IITB who worked on this research while he was in IIML), and Professor Pankaj Kumar (IIML). My colleagues at MDI, Dr Arun Kumar (now on the faculty at IIT-Chennai), Dr Subir Verma (professor, MDI Gurgaon), and Dr Swati Nalawade (now freelance consultant in Bombay) deserve special mention for going out of their way to help me with data collection in different business schools. Needless to say, this study would not have seen the light of day without the kind support of the directors of the schools under study—Professor Bakul Dholakia (Former Director IIM-Ahmedabad), Professor Shekhar Chaudhury (Former Director IIM-Calcutta), Professor Prakash Apte (Former Director IIM-Bangalore), Dr Sen Gupta, (Former Director S P Jain Institute of Management and Research-Mumbai), Father Abraham (Former Director XIM-Bhubaneswar), and Father N Casimir Raj, S. J. (Former Director XLRI-Jamshedpur).

Special thanks go out to senior corporate executives and alumni who participated in this study and shared their views. Vindy Banga, Former Chairman of Hindustan Lever Limited (HLL), P. Dwarakanath,

Former Head of Human Resources at GlaxoSmithKline (GSK), Satish Pradhan (Head HR-Tata Sons), Dr Santrupt Misra (Head HR-Aditya Birla Group), Arvind Agarwal, Head of HR R P Goenka (RPG) Group, Marcel Parker (Head HR-Raymond), S P Agarwal (Ferguson), Pramath Sinha (Former partner of McKinsey), G P Rao GM–HR from the then Juggilal Kamlapat (JK) Group, Prem Kamath (Head HR-ex HLL), Pradeep Mukerjee (Head HR-CitiGroup), and a host of senior corporate executives, spared valuable time for discussions, thereby adding rich insights from the corporate perspective.

Special heartfelt thanks go to the members of my research support team at MDI—Hemant Bathla, Nitin Jindal, Rachit Kalia, Suneera Bhattacharya, Vasudha Lamba, and Vikram Sharma—for relentlessly working right from the questionnaire development stage to data analysis to completing this gigantic work. Thanks Pranav and thanks, Gurudatt for all your help.

Finally, I would like to thank Sugata Ghosh and his team at SAGE publications, for their interest in and support of this project as well as for their responsiveness.

3 April 2007

Asha Bhandarker
MDI-Gurgaon

Chapter 1
Building future business leaders

THE RESEARCH LITERATURE

Introduction

The business context has undergone a drastic shift with the advent of globalization, new paradigms of business, and the IT-led transformations, which have enormously impacted corporate sector functioning. Indeed, this is the age of discontinuity and tectonic shifts. One can clearly experience the confluence of ambiguity, uncertainties, and complexities. Capra's prophetic book, *Thriving on Chaos* and Andy Grove's, *Only the Paranoid Survive* are a telling commentary on the sheer velocity of the turbulence hitting businesses. The hyper-competition unfolding in the global context has thrown up many new challenges threatening the very survival of organizations and rendering the current business scenario into an Olympiad, where only the fittest survive (Singh and Bhandarker 2002).

Increasingly, India is becoming the new arena for global competition where the biggest corporate battles will be fought. Indian businesses of tomorrow will need managers and leaders who can thrive amidst the challenges of living and working in a global world; who can cope with challenges of a chaotic business world; and who can deal with the demand for continued change and improvement. More and more corporate leaders will have to prepare to operate in a global world characterized by diversity, absorb and deal with the continuous technological innovations, as well as balance the same with the increasingly conflicting needs of business and society. Indian businesses need leaders who can relentlessly create the second curve, navigate with kaleidoscopic vision, and prepare organizations to cope with the ambiguities, uncertainties, and complexity.

The history of economic development powerfully brings out that the prosperity of a nation is not necessarily linked with the availability of natural resources. It has been decisively proved that talent plays a critical role in the development and prosperity of a nation. Fortunately, this is the area where India has a crucial competitive advantage over most other nations. Worldwide, when nations like USA, China, Japan, Canada, and various European countries would be grey (by 2020), India will have a 325 million strong population aged between 25 and 35 years. Thus, India would emerge as the sourcing hub for human resources and the world will look to India for high-quality talent.

If we rise to meet this demand and train our youth on relevant knowledge and skills in higher education, they will be able to take advantage of job opportunities[1] and the 21st century will indeed be the Indian century. If we fail to rise up to this challenge, however, India will miss another golden leadership opportunity. Movement of outsourced jobs to India over the last decade suggests that jobs are available for those with higher education. Even within India, the remarkable rise of cities like Pune, Bangalore, Hyderabad, Delhi, and Chennai exemplify this fact. In order to become one of the powerful global economies in 2020[2], India will have to develop focused policies for education, especially higher education and research. Indian higher education policy and the strategies of institutions of higher education need to be aligned with the global demands and challenges to actualize the opportunities, in order to emerge as the hub for future global leaders in business.

One may examine the policy of the country in the emerging context and also study the strategic thrust of institutes of higher education. However in the present research, the focus is restricted to post graduate Management Education in India's top schools. The objective is to understand the level of fit between educational strategies of the schools vis-à-vis the quality of business leaders which tomorrow's world needs.

Management Education has a tremendous role to play in grooming future business leaders in tune with the requirements thrown up by changes in the context. In fact, the strengths of an achieving society (in the fields of commerce, business, and trade) lie in its intellectual prowess, continuous technological and product innovation, and constant learning orientation. These competitive capabilities and mindsets emanate from long-term commitment to improve quality of life, national emphasis on knowledge building, and high quality of education. It is no coincidence that achieving societies have laid great emphasis on knowledge creation and nurtured high quality academic institutions in the field of business education—for example, INSEAD in France, London Business School and Cranfield School of Business in the UK, McGill in Canada, Kellogg, Wharton, Stanford, Harvard, and others in the USA. These countries have invested considerable resources in developing and nurturing these institutions.

Management thinkers consider shaping talent and developing future business leaders to be one of the key objectives of B-Schools education (Bharuch and Leeming 1996, Sheridan 1993, Doyle 1992, and Roth 1990); this view has also been echoed by the corporate sector. In fact, corporate executives (interviewed for this research study) have gone to the extent of saying that they come to recruit from top schools because 'these schools groom future leaders'.

Management Education has been at the receiving end of criticism from the corporate sector for not adequately aligning themselves with industry requirements and developing analysts rather than managers. The debate on the role of management education and the need to reorient it with a view to build business leaders has been around for many decades now. In USA, there have been three major efforts to assess the state of business education (*Gordon and Howell* report and *Pierson* Report—both published in the year 1959, Porter and McKibbin 1988). Similar efforts were also made in the UK (Handy 1988 and *Frank Report* 1963) as well as Australia (Selen 2001 and Martin 1996) and India (Dayal 2001, Sheth 1992, Satia 1992, Philip 1992, and Baumgartel 1986). All these studies have emphatically raised concerns regarding the quality and relevance of B-School education.

The Porter and McKibbin (1988) survey of US schools, as well as recruiting companies brought out:

1. The need for management schools to develop leadership and interpersonal skills among B-School graduates,
2. Provide them with greater practical orientation, and
3. Maintain closer interactions and ties with the business community.

Although many schools are making the required changes in their curricula, triggered by the Porter and McKibbin recommendations, concerns continue to be raised (Prince and Stewart 2000 and Deutschman 1991). Jacobson's (1993) research brought out that MBAs were perceived as lacking in basic skills of management which are needed to be effective business leaders.

Management thinkers (Bennis and Toole 2006 and Mintzberg 2001) have highlighted that execution and people management are poorly developed among MBAs. In fact, Mintzberg goes on to say 'Execution is about context, about depth of understanding of specific business and industry in question ... people ... get short shrift on MBA programmes because the tendency is to equate managing with analytical decision making'. Assessment of the values of graduates from leading schools as well as the extent to which they have changed through B-School inputs and experience is another line of research. Krishnan's study (2003) reveals a shift from 'Other oriented' to 'Self oriented' values among the graduates after the B-School programme. Value erosion has also been reported by Schneider (2002) and raises concerns regarding the impact of B-Schools on value orientation of B-School graduates. The well-known Aspen (2001) study across top American schools showed that B-School graduates assign greater priority to maximizing shareholder value (after B-School experience) rather than high-quality goods and services, corporate social responsibility, and environmental sensitivity. Such findings clearly bring out that B-School exposure tends to make graduates more self oriented, while the other oriented values like customerization, environmental sensitivity, and social responsibility get lower priority.

THE INDIAN CONTEXT OF MANAGEMENT EDUCATION

Management schools have been operating in India for more than four decades. The earliest school to be set up in India was IIM-Ahmedabad (in collaboration with Harvard Business School) and IIM-Calcutta (in collaboration with MIT Sloan School of Management) in the early 1960s. In fact, the last decade has seen a proliferation of schools recognized by the All India Council for Technical Education (AICTE) in the country (approximately 1200). Today, there is a plethora of B-Schools ranging from Super League (top 10) as well as Big League schools (next 10) and tapering all the way down to purely commercial ventures, which thrive given the insatiable demand for professional education for a burgeoning youthful population. In fact, it is a matter of concern that the tail is alarmingly longer than the list of good schools.

Examination of the global ranking of B-Schools shows that, none of the top Indian Schools feature among the top 20 schools world-wide. It is indeed a sad commentary that on the one hand we have around 1200 schools and on the other hand, not a single one of them has attained global stature. Although some schools have been tinkering with the curriculum over the last few years, by and large however even in the leading schools, the business education paradigm has stayed more or less unchanged for many decades, focusing more on developing intellectual power rather than building leaders. B-Schools in India are typically criticized for

1. not being upto global standards and
2. not meeting expectations of the corporate world.

Given this context, it is pertinent to ask the question: Are B-Schools actually playing their roles and developing managers and future leaders with the needed competencies, mindsets, attitude, and behavioural profiles or are they mere filtration points, where top quality talent enters the schools based on their performance on the Common Admission Test (CAT) and subsequently land the best jobs based on brand value of the top schools? Is there any substantial value addition by the business school in developing leaders?

B-School education in India, unlike the US and Europe, is open to graduates without work experience. Top schools in the US attract people with an average of five years of work experience. In India, even in the top schools, there is a significantly large percentage of people without work experience. Even those who do have work experience typically have an average of 2–3 years. The task of developing managerial competencies is therefore even more daunting in the Indian B-School context.

There is also the corporate context where long induction periods are being rethought. Corporate executives (in our research) affirm that unlike the past, today they are becoming increasingly specific regarding their competency requirements and expect B-Schools to provide these (competencies) to the graduates, since companies are increasingly strapped for time.

Researchers Dayal (2001), Sheth (1992), Baumgartel (1986), have been highlighting the need to revamp the educational inputs in Indian B-Schools. Closer scrutiny however indicates there have been few holistic efforts to assess and remodel B-School education, making it more relevant to the needs of stakeholders—students, and corporate sector. Even the best schools appear to be complacent and sitting pretty on their past success and brand value rather than striving to be closely connected and responsive to the requirements of the key stakeholders. A professor from a long established and respected school said, 'Despite everything, top quality students will continue to flock to us and corporates will have to come to us anyway, so where is the problem?' This statement sums up the attitude of many B-Schools in India today. In fact, most Indian B-Schools use placements and salaries as a badge of honour to highlight their superiority as compared to other schools. Very few schools take pride in and talk about the methods and pedagogies they use to shape the perspective and thinking of the students; the world class research they undertake; or their contribution to stakeholders through high impact consulting work and Management Development Programmes (MDPs) which they conduct. No wonder they are viewed like employment exchanges by both, corporates and students.

The unending debate on Management Education is an outcome of the typical, academic, input-focused approach to delivering education rather than focusing on building the needed competencies to prepare students for the managerial roles for which they are being prepared. Needless to say, this unending debate will continue unless B-Schools adopt appropriate pedagogy to bring symbioses of conceptual input with a pragmatic and action orientation.

Examination of the educational models in other professional courses like Medical and Legal—indicates that they have a strong practice component—observation and work at laboratories, hospitals, and the court—unlike Management Education where the practise component is conspicuous by its absence. It is no wonder then that management schools are not inculcating managerial competencies of execution, influence, and mobilization essential to the business of management. The above analysis raises the following broad questions about Management Education in India:

1. Does Management Education have an impact on shaping and grooming the graduates?
2. Do they have an impact on development of needed managerial competencies, attitudes, and mindsets? Or
3. Are management schools mere filtration points to sift high quality talent at the entry stage?

THE RESEARCH LITERATURE

There has been a perennial quest to identify the competencies which contribute to the making of a leader. Thinkers (Blake and Mouton 1964; Burns 2003; Singh and Bhandarker 1990, 1994; Bossidy and Charan 2002; Avolio 1999; Kotter 1999; Bennis 1997; Yukl 1997; House 1996, 1977, 1973; Kouzes and Posner 1995; Schein 1992; Yammarino and Bass 1990; Conger 1989;

Conger and Kanungo 1988; Tichy and Devanna 1986; Bass 1985; Bennis and Nanus 1985; Stogdill and Bass 1981; Greenleaf 1977; Hersey and Blanchard 1977; Argyris 1976; Zaleznik 1977; Fiedler 1967; Bowers and Seashore 1996; and McGregor 1966) have identified a host of capabilities—task, people as well as team orientation, context centric and opportunity-sensing mindset, diversity management, entrepreneurship and risk taking, transformational zeal, passion and fervour to contribute etc., relevant for effective leadership. Of late, however, there has been an increased emphasis on competencies like complexity management, diversity management, managing self, influencing and mobilizing others, building vision and architecting organization, global mindset, entrepreneurial mindset, and innovation management to be an effective leader in the emerging business landscape.

In this study, four clusters have been selected broadly encompassing many of the above competencies relevant for shaping the leadership potential of the MBA graduates:

1.   The first cluster—Intrapersonal—consists of attributes like Emotional Self Awareness, Emotional Awareness of Others, Intentionality, Resilience, Optimism, and Empathy.

2. The second cluster—Influencing Others—comprises Emotional Expression, Interpersonal Connection, Constructive Discontent, and Trust.
3. The third cluster—Managing Complexity—consists of Intuition and Creativity.
4. The fourth cluster—Managing Diversity—constitutes Tolerance of Ambiguity and Flexibility.

These clusters have also been extensively examined under the domain of Emotional Intelligence, as well as personality and are considered precursors to effective leadership.

The literature on Intra-personal and Interpersonal competencies; Managing Complexity and Diversity Management, and their relevance for leadership have been examined in the subsequent analyses.

Intrapersonal competencies: Self management and self regulation

Through millennia, political thinkers, philosophers, and religious leaders have emphasized the power of Knowing Self, Owning Self, and Changing Self, for Managing Self and others. Management thinkers (Boyatzis et al. 2002, Kotter 1999, Bennis 1997, Segal 1997,

Hogan et al. 1994, and Chin and Kenneth 1984) have also emphasized this. Many leaders—Mussolini, Stalin, Saddam Hussain, Hitler, Popescu, Nixon, etc., were derailed, not because of their poor capability to mobilize people, but because of their incapability to manage themselves. Those leaders who managed themselves well (in addition to their other leadership capabilities)—Gandhi, Mandela, Roosevelt, Gorbachev, Lincoln—went on to become outstanding leaders, and made a positive difference to society at large.

Self management is thus an important requirement for leaders, who have to manage not only their own hopes, failures, fears but also that of their followers. Self management constitutes capability to understand, regulate and manage oneself. Self management and self regulation are an outcome of self awareness and self understanding.

In this section we examine the research on Self Awareness, Optimism, and Resilience, the three attributes contributing to self management and self regulation.

Self awareness

It is widely accepted that enhanced Self Awareness leads to increased effectiveness at work (Bernardin 1986 and Burke et al. 1985). It is found to be associated with Transformational Leadership (Sosik and Megerian

1999); and distinguishes between star performers and others (Kelley 1998). Self Awareness has been found to contribute to superior performance (Goleman 1998, Boyatzis 1982); managerial and career development (Chen 1998 and Amundson 1995); achieving managerial excellence, high performance and effectiveness, as well as perceived effectiveness ratings by peers and supervisors (Church and Waclawski 1999, Church 1997, Shipper and Dillard 1994, Tornow 1993, Van Velsor et al. 1993, Atwater and Yammarino 1992, and Ashford and Tsui 1991). High potential managers have been found to be more self aware, as compared to average potential managers (Church 1997). Individuals with high levels of Self Awareness are in a better position to respond proactively to external circumstances and exert more control over long-term effects (Amundson 1995: 11). In fact, self awareness is an important first step to development of interpersonal skills (Koen and Crow 1995). Needless to say, interpersonal skills are basic to influencing others.

Optimism

Optimism is an important attribute which helps maintain hope regardless of the situation. Many researchers (Chang 2001, Gillham 2000, Schulman 1999 and Seligman 1990), have examined Optimism and its impact on behaviour. Research has brought out that Optimism contributes to better Self Management (Schulman 1995); inspires problem solving (Abramson et al. 1978); academic achievement and job productivity (Schulman 1995); and greater health (Peterson 1988). In fact, Transformational leaders are found to be higher on Optimism (Spreitzer and Quinn 1996) as compared to others.

Resilience

Resilience has been defined as the, 'tendency to recover from or adjust easily to misfortune or change' (Merriam-Webster's Online Dictionary 2005). The capacity to recover and bounce back in the face of difficult situations is an essential requirement to deal with tough and unpredictable business challenges. High performing insurance salesmen have been found to be more resilient and optimistic than managers and even world class athletes (Stoltz 2000 and Schulman 1999). There is a long tradition of research on resilience in the face of adversity (Sylvester et al. 2003, Proudfoot et al. 2001, Corr and Gray 1996, Stoltz 1996, Seligman and Schulman 1986, and Maddi and Kobasa 1984). It has been found that a hardy personality (Maddi and Kobasa 1984) who is resilient, self reliant, with zest for life, is able to cope with anxieties and risks. Such people have a vigorous sense of commitment, control and challenge and tend to react positively to stressful events. It is possible to conclude that future leaders must develop capability at self management before they can manage others.

Interpersonal competencies

Interpersonal competency has been conceptualized by researchers (Boyatzis 2000; Goleman 1998; Bar-On 1997; Spencer and Spencer 1993) as the ability to connect with people, understand, and influence them. Such competency forms the basic foundation for building teams and bonding with people which enables organizational goal achievement. Some of the prominent interpersonal attributes contributing to leadership effectiveness are:

1. Ability to establish Interpersonal connection; establishing goodwill (Gregersen et al. 1998),
2. Relationship Management (Brake 1997),
3. Inspire others to action, effective listener and communicator, ability to transform conflict into creative action (Rosen et al. 2000),
4. Empowerment (Kets de Vries and Mead 1992), and
5. Interpersonal Sensitivity (Gardner 1999).

Interpersonal competencies like relationship building (Boyatzis 1996, Spencer and Spencer 1993, and McClelland 1973); empathy (Bar-On 2000; Orioli et al. 2000 and Goleman 1998); interpersonal understanding and team work (Fetzer Consortium, cited in Goleman 1998, Spencer and Spencer 1993 and McClelland 1973); managing conflict (Fetzer Consortium 1998 and Goleman 1998); understanding others (Orioli et al. 2000 and Goleman 1998); communication/emotional expression (Orioli et al. 2000 and Goleman 1998); building bonds/interpersonal connection/interpersonal relationships (Gowing 2001, Orioli et al. 2000, Bar-On 2000, and Goleman 1998) have been extensively studied for effective leadership. Studies on managerial failures (McCall et al. 1988 and Bentz 1985) have brought out that such managers were unable to maintain relationships and build teams, thus highlighting the importance of good interpersonal influence capabilities for managerial effectiveness.

Four interpersonal behaviours relevant for effective leadership were identified as follows—empathy, understanding the needs of others, trust, and influence—and have been well researched. Studies (Kellet et al. 2002, Wolff et al. 2002) have brought out that those who display empathy have a better chance of emerging as leaders.

According to Humphrey's (2002) review of research, managing group emotion is one of the major routes to leader influence. According to Pescolido (2002), members high in empathy will be more likely to engage in management of emotion. Empathy has been found to correlate with effective sales (Eroglu and Pilling 1994). Building emotional bonds has been found to be an integral part of Transformational Leadership (Barbuto and Burbach 2006). Further, research has brought out that leaders who successfully manage group processes can substantially influence performance. Ability to understand the needs of others (another interpersonal attribute) has been found to characterize the best managers of product development teams (Spencer and Spencer 1993). Trust is considered to be an essential ingredient for developing cooperation in groups (Coleman 1988, Jones and George 1998, and McAllister 1995) and this is important in the light of the fact that cooperation and collaboration have been established as basic for group effectiveness (Druskat and Wolff 2001: 133–134). In fact, Roy and Dugal (1998) conclude from their literature review that interpersonal trust is important for sustaining individual and organizational effectiveness. Thus, in contemporary business organizations, influencing others is considered to be one of the critical leadership competencies.

MANAGING COMPLEXITY (FLUX UNCERTAINTY AND CHANGE) IN THE BUSINESS CONTEXT

Future leaders will be faced with the overwhelming challenge of operating in the complex environment generated by the pace and scale of change and the need to move seamlessly across different situations, cultures, as well as interact with different kinds of people. In fact, business leaders of today need to be like the seafarers of the great oceans who successfully navigated without reliable maps, in dangerous waters, with storms looming large on the horizon.

Today's business is characterized by brutal storm of competitors, seemingly strange cultures, endless business horizons, confusing marketing channels and unknown frontiers of technology (Gregersen et al. 1998) In such an age of discontinuity, business leaders need to develop alert antenna, build opportunity-sensing mindset and have the courage to go beyond the set rules and frameworks in order to successfully navigate the present. Thus in the contemporary business world, we need leaders with entrepreneurial zeal, curiosity, and enthusiasm to create new routes.

Management thinkers and gurus consider open and flexible mindset (Rhinesmith 1996), unbridled inquisitiveness and ability to embrace duality (Gregersen et al. 1998), curiosity, constant learning (Brake 1997), concern with context and acceptance of complexity and its contradictions (Rosen et al. 2000 and Srinivas 1995) as some of the required attributes to thrive in the global context. This section examines two critical attributes—intuition and creativity—relevant to manage complexity.

Intuition

In the Jungian typology, the intuitive person 'concentrates on the possibilities and is less concerned with details... finds solutions directly without basing them on facts' (cited by Andersen 2000: 6). Researchers have conclusively proved the importance of Intuition for managing complexity (Dane and Pratt 2007: 8, Hogarth 2001, Andersen 2000, Khatri and Ng 2000, Burke and Miller 1999, and Agor 1986). The need for Intuition is especially acute in contemporary organizations operating in turbulent business contexts. Creative use of Intuition has been found to be a critical differentiator between successful and non-successful top executives and board members (Dane and Pratt 2007). Intuition is a non-conscious process and involves making holistic associations (Dane and Pratt 2007). Persons using intuition are found to be fast and quick decision makers (Dane and Pratt 2007). According to Hogarth (2001), there is a powerful association between emotion and intuitive thought.

Khatri and Ng (2000) have extensively studied the usage of Intuition in decision making across banking, utilities, and computer sectors. Their findings bring out that gut feel (intuition) is used more for strategic decision making in the computer industry as compared to the others. Similarly, Agor's study (1986) reveals the preponderant usage of Intuition for strategic decision making. Dane and Pratt's (2007) work also brings out that Intuition is integral to successfully completing tasks characterized by high complexity and short time horizon.

Studies (Khatri and Ng 2000 and Burke and Miller 1999) have sought to examine the use of Intuition by managers for the purpose of decision making. In a study of strategic decision making (Khatri and Ng 2000) by 281 senior-level managers from 221 companies across computers, banking, and utilities, use of 'gut feel' for strategic decision making was much more in the computer industry than in banking or utilities. The context in which Intuition gets used for decision making is very relevant—in a study of 60 professionals (Burke and Miller 1999) it was found that intuition is used when decisions need to be made quickly or under conditions of uncertainty and also when situations did not have clear clues. Research shows that managers use Intuition for strategic decision making (Agor 1986). Research suggests that intuition may be integral to successfully completing tasks that involve high complexity and short time horizons (Dane and Pratt 2007).

In 'Untangling the Intuition Mess: Intuition as a Construct in Entrepreneurship Research', Mitchell et al. (2005) reviewed the literature and brought out that there is a strong association of intuition with creativity and innovation, with new market learning (Crossan et al. 1999 and Hisrich and Jankowicz 1990), improvement of competitiveness (Lank and Lank 1995 and Behling and Eckel 1991), opportunity recognition (Allinson et al. 2000), improved organizational performance (Covin et al. 2001 and Khatri and Ng 2000), and rapid or more efficient decision making (Allinson et al. 2000, Burke and Miller 1999, Bennett 1998, Simon 1987).

Creativity

Every business experiences cycles of change. Businesses have to undergo the phase of growth, consolidation, and possible decay. Thus every business has to continually cope with uncertainties and threats to its growth and survival. As competition increases, business cycles get shorter. The demand for new strategic positioning, new markets and products become imperative for survival and growth even to maintain status quo. In today's business scenario, standing still is akin to moving backwards because competitors continuously strive to move forward. It is in this context that creativity is considered to be a key factor for organizational competitiveness.

Creativity is 'the production of novel, appropriate ideas in any realm of human activity. Ideas must be novel and they must be appropriate to the problem or opportunity presented (Amabile 1997). Creativity has been viewed as the first step to Innovation...' the successful implementation of those novel, appropriate ideas.

Successful entrepreneurs are found to be high on creativity (Bolin 1997). In the last couple of decades Amabile and her students (1985, 1986, 1987—see 1997) have been extensively studying the phenomenon of individual and organizational creativity. Creative thinking has been found to be related to a cluster of personality attributes like independence, self discipline, ambiguity tolerance, perseverance, orientation to risk taking, and relative lack of concern for social approval (Amabile 1997: 5). There is some evidence (Pinard and Allio 2005 and McFadzean 1998) indicating that creativity can be enhanced. In a recent study (Heames and Service 2003) of employers of MBA graduates of Babson College, most of the sample (above 90 per cent) rated the ability to develop creative solutions as very important for successful job performance.

The above findings on Creativity and Intuition clearly bring out their relevance for managing complexity. In fact, they are found to be the bedrock for managing complexity. In other words, creative and innovative leaders will be much more effective for managing in the age of discontinuity.

Diversity management—managing in global context

Today, business is truly global and this is reflected in the profiles of customers, suppliers, and employees. The phenomenon of internationalization of business is amply illustrated by two kinds of data:

1. It has been reported (Rosen et al. 2000) that in the customers category the highest percentage of international customers, relatively speaking, is in Europe (83 per cent), the lowest is from North America (57 per cent);

2. Likewise, similar pattern is evident in the case of international suppliers and employees. This profoundly reveals the simple fact of seamlessness of marketing and borderlessness of the world, hence rendering the globe truly interconnected. Gregersen et al. (1998) studied Fortune 500 companies and concluded that 85 per cent of these companies' executives expressed that organizations need greater percentage of managers with a global mindset. Sixty seven per cent of the interviewed executives of these firms however felt that those operating as global leaders do not have the required capability, and also expressed that there is a felt need to heighten the same.

The power of a nation is thus moving from the state to the market. It is a paradox that while on the one hand the world is becoming borderless, on the other hand, there is resurgence of human quest for identity manifested through emergence of ethnic, religious, and cultural consciousness. This has made the world full of contradictions, the economic forces driving the globe towards convergence; while the socio-cultural and political forces are striving for establishing unique identity. In order to successfully operate in a scenario full of apparently contradictory forces, the business world needs leaders with a capacity to manage diversity.

Management thinkers (Gregersen et al. 1998, Morgan 1998, Rosen and Brown 1996, Srinivas 1995, Moran and Reisenberger 1994, Kets de Vries and Mead 1992, Prahalad and Hamel 1990, and Bartlett and Ghoshal 1992) make a strong case for developing a distinctively different mindset and competencies to operate in a global context, as compared to operating in the local context. Leaders of today must build a global mindset characterized by drive for a broader picture, ability to balance contradictions, engage process, flow with change, value diversity, and lead globally (Rhinesmith 1996). While Kets de Vries and Mead (1992) emphasize the importance of cultural adaptability, Moran and Reisenberger (1994) stress the importance of ability to profile cultures and gather knowledge of and respect for other countries, ability to work with multi-cultural teams and work as an equal with persons from diverse backgrounds. While talking about global leadership, Morgan (1998) emphasized openness to learn from experience as well as continuous knowledge and learning updation. Diversity consciousness and sensitivity (Srinivas 1995) have also been emphasized as important attributes for future leaders. Research (Gregersen et al. 1998) has revealed that individuals on international assignments are characterized by greater curiosity, open mindedness, sense of adventure, and inquisitiveness.

Gupta and Govindrajan (2002) highlight the need for both cognitive diversity as well as integrative ability.

According to Percy Barnevik (1991), 'Global managers have exceptionally open minds. They respect how different cultures do things and have the imagination to appreciate why they do them that way....'

From the previous discussion, one may conclude that to thrive in today's world with its diverse and contradictory forces, business leaders need to develop high degree of flexibility and tolerance of ambiguity.

Flexibility

Flexibility is an attitude characterized by a ready capability to adapt to new, different, or changing requirements (Merriam-Webster Online dictionary 2005). Flexibility is essential to operate in changing circumstances and for managing diversity of people and ideas. Flexibility has been identified as an important capability by researchers (Fetzer Consortium, cited in Goleman 1998; Bar-On 2000; Boyatzis 2000; and McClelland 1973). Emerging leadership theories (Boal and Whitehead 1992) highlight that cognitive and behavioural complexity and flexibility are important characteristics of competent leaders. Successful leaders have been found to be more adaptable to changes in the external environment especially in the international context (Spreitzer et al. 1997). Those who are high on ambiguity tolerance are also found to be more adaptable (Kirton 1976) as well as being more flexible (Kirton 1981). Research on rigidity (the opposite of flexibility) and its correlates gives us some insight into the nature of flexibility. Rigidity has been found to be positively correlated with intolerance of ambiguity (Mishra 1995). Originality has been found to be negatively correlated with intolerance of ambiguity, inflexibility, and positively correlated with extraversion (Kirton 1976).

Tolerance—Intolerance of ambiguity (TIA)

Global leaders embrace duality by managing uncertainty, essentially knowing when to act and when to gather more information and balancing tensions, understanding what needs to change and what needs to stay the same from country to country and region to region (Gregersen et al. 1998). This highlights the importance of higher tolerance of ambiguity (that is lower intolerance of ambiguity) for managing in situations of uncertainty created by changing business context as well as by complexity.

The concept of Ambiguity Tolerance has been operationalized and measured by researchers on a continuum from Low Intolerance (that is Ambiguity Tolerance) to High Intolerance of Ambiguity, as indicated in the studies discussed hereafter.

Budner (1962) defined Intolerance of Ambiguity as the 'tendency to perceive ambiguous situations as a source of threat' (Budner 1962). Studies have shown that Intolerance of Ambiguity is positively associated with rigidity (Kehman and Barclay 1969, Akhtar and Singh 1972, Zacker 1973), as well as with adapter orientation (Kirton 1981). Low Intolerance of Ambiguity has been found to correlate positively with creativity. A study on Irish managers, Barron (1969) found that those with high scores on originality were more comfortable with complexity and uncertainty. His research also brought out that highly inflexible people tend to be low on originality, more rigid and also more intolerant of ambiguity.

Lower Intolerance of Ambiguity has been found to be a characteristic of entrepreneurs (Schere 1982, Sexton and Bowman 1984). Entrepreneurs have been found to be more comfortable with novelty and complexity as compared to managers (Beglerp and Boyd 1986). In fact, entrepreneurs have been profiled as people with a liking for uncertainty and change. Entrepreneurially inclined students have been found to have greater innovativeness, more ambiguity tolerance, and higher propensity to take risks, as compared to those who are not entrepreneurially inclined (Koh 1996). Most entrepreneurial firms in a Spanish study (Entrialgo et al. 2000) across 233 firms were found to be managed by individuals with greater locus of control, higher need for achievement and greater tolerance of ambiguity. In a study of Indians managers, it was found that they are moderate on ambiguity tolerance (Singh et al. 1996). Similar findings emerged in another Indian study (Nalini 1999).

Tolerance of Ambiguity assumes importance in a scenario characterized by diversity, complexity, and uncertainty. It is equally important where the context is dynamic and change is the order of the day. In most business settings, such a phenomenon is increasingly a way of life. Only a leader, who can deal with diversity, multiplicity, and ambiguity, with ability to create a structure out of the fluidity, would be able to lead effectively and move faster than the competitors. In contrast, those who find it difficult to operate without structure and framework, those with low ambiguity tolerance, would find it very difficult to thrive in today's chaotic and diverse scenario. Higher ambiguity tolerance is indicative of the highest level of cognitive development (Loevinger 1976: 24–25). It is associated with increased conceptual complexity and ability to deal with complex patterns.

From the discussion so far, one can conclude that today's world needs leaders with greater tolerance of ambiguity and flexibility.

The key thrust of this research is on understanding and assessing the development of future leaders by some leading Indian business schools. In the present work, leadership has been viewed as an influence process, the sources of which can be connected to three key domains—cognitive (ability to analyze and reason), conative (involving will and resolve), and affective (involving feelings, vision, values, hope, trust, compassion). The most powerful of the three is emotional power, which is critical for connecting with people and influencing them (of course, this does not mean that intellectual capability is not important, rather it means there is great need to also develop the other influencing modes). This has been very visible in great leaders like Gandhi, Lincoln, and Mandela who have used this power extensively and mobilized people. When cognitive, conative and affective powers are used together, the result can be a phenomenal leadership force which can achieve the seemingly impossible.

The major leadership crisis facing human society is linked to the fact that while the intellectual development of a human being is steeply on the ascendant (and getting very highly developed as at no other time in human history), development of emotional intelligence has simply not kept pace. In fact the trend of nuclear families, the increasing fragility of marriage as an institution, the rise in individualism, have contributed to under development of many aspects of emotional intelligence. Some of the emotional intelligence skills demonstrated by earlier generations may be virtually lost in modern and post modern societies. The paradox, however, is that people get inspired and are willing to stretch themselves when they are touched on the emotional level, feel in sync with the meaning they find in the organization, which invariably has the leader playing a critical role directly or indirectly. A recent research (Singh, Jain and Bhandarker 2006) brought out that young Indians in their thirties, look for fulfillment of many needs in the workplace including social, esteem, and spiritual needs, highlighting the criticality of the leadership role in addressing and taking care of these needs.

In fact, the ancient and evergreen wisdom from Confucius to *Bhishma* emphasize the important qualities to be looked for in a potential king (leader)—He who 'has dreams for the Future, Sense of Purpose, Soul Sensitivity, and Compassion'. Leadership is about building bonds between leaders and the people. This bonding is rooted more in emotional and spiritual power than either intellectual power or action power alone.

Leading American Business schools are seeking to move beyond the over emphasis on intellectual development, and experimenting with developing leadership competencies. Further, the emphasis is also moving towards issues of corporate social responsibility and ethics. Clearly, these are matters not of the intellectual domain but lie more in the emotional and spiritual domains.

As mentioned earlier, management schools are criticized for their inability to develop leaders with the requisite ability to influence teams, build personal touch as well as convert ideas into action. In addition, there is paucity of empirical evidence which can provide insights about this phenomenon. In fact, no major study has been undertaken in India after Baumgartel's work two decades ago (1986). This was another reason why I felt the need to take up this research work.

The study seeks to identify the leadership competencies appropriate for the emerging context discussed above. Sensitivity to understand the contextual demands and link the same with leadership competencies is one of the critical challenges for a B-School. Preparing students in alignment with these requirements will aid in development of graduates, known not only for their intellectual capability but also their capability to connect with people, influence and lead; boldly go ahead in complex contexts and look for creative solutions to issues and challenges.

The basic model underlying the work is presented in Figure 1.1:

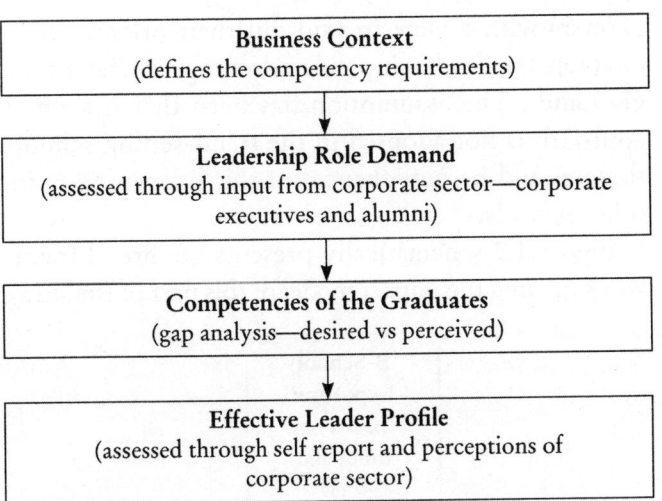

Figure 1.1 **Effective leader profile—a context based approach**

ABOUT THE STUDY

This study has been conducted in two parts:

Part 1: Assessment of the Psychometric Approach profile

This part of the study is a longitudinal work conducted at two stages—data was gathered from the graduates at the entry stage into the B-Schools and also at the exit stage. We deliberately chose the Super League schools

(Top 9) with a view to find out their orientation to develop the leadership related competencies of the graduates. The assumption has been that if such an approach is not adopted in the trend-setting schools, there would be dim chances of this happening in the other schools.

Figure 1.2 schematically presents the broad framework guiding the impact model of this part of the study.

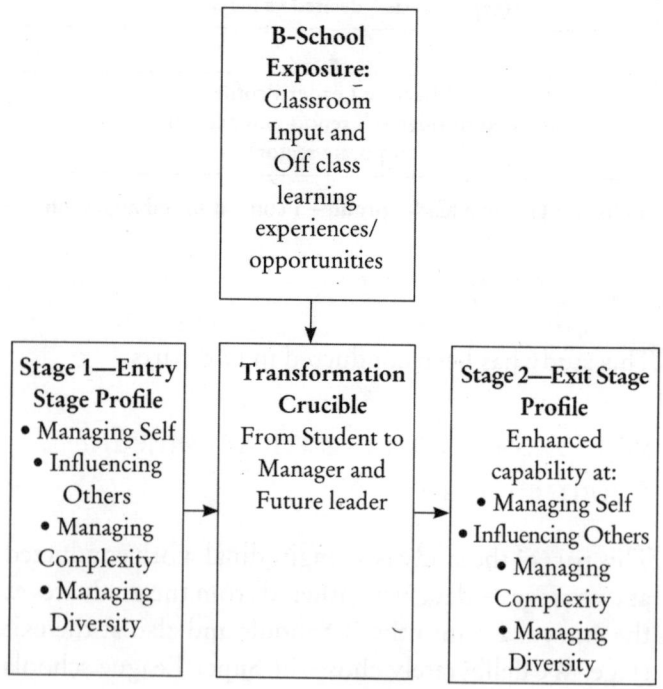

Figure 1.2 **B-School education—impact assessment**

The specific competency requirements for future leaders which emerged in the above literature review have been classified and presented below (for details of measurement—definitions, scale properties, and factor analytical justification for the four competency clusters assessed in the study see Appendices 1 to 3). These have been assessed through a psychometric approach and constitute:

1. *Self Management*—the ability of self awareness and self understanding, which in turn helps in regulating one's emotions; retain optimism, maintain sense of self confidence with ability to cope with difficult situations, without losing focus.

2. *Influencing Others*—The capability to identify the emotional state of others, develop rapport with them, work in teams, constructively manage conflict by using the power of trust and express relevant emotions as and when appropriate.

3. *Managing Diversity*—The ability to cope with diversity of views, ideas, and opinions through a tolerance of differences as well as the flexibility to be open to different viewpoints.

4. *Managing Complexity*—The ability to be open minded in complex and new situations, using the power of intuition, exploring and thinking beyond the known frameworks, and arriving at creative solutions to complex problems.

Table 1.1 Needed competencies for effective leadership

Competencies	Cluster of attributes assessed in this research
Managing Diversity	Flexibility; Tolerance-Intolerance of ambiguity
Managing Complexity	Creativity; Intuition;
Self-management Intrapersonal competencies for Self management and Self Regulation	Resilience; Self Awareness; Emotional Awareness of Others; Intentionality; Optimism
Influencing Others Interpersonal competencies for managing and influencing people	Emotional Expression, Interpersonal Connection, Constructive discontent and Trust;

Notes: Competencies—Based on the literature review.
Attributes—Personality trait, attitude, skill and/or value

Pilot testing

The psychometric tests were adapted (primarily changes in language, especially the use of colloquial English) based on detailed discussions with a sample of 35 students representing the target group.

Sample and data collection

Business schools were selected for the semi-longitudinal study, on the basis of the ranking by Business World in the year 2000. Although each year many ranking lists are published, we opted for this one since it was one of the qualitatively better surveys. Thus, students of schools which featured in the top ten ranks were considered. Nine of the top schools participated in the study. However, one school—FMS—declined to participate. For the purpose of this study, this group is called the Super-League schools.

Super league schools

Round 1: Data collection was done in July and August 2001 (within the first 2 months of the students having joined the post graduate programme). One thousand two hundred and eighty six students participated in Round 1.

Round 2: Data collection took place in the same schools and on the same sample the following year. (Table 2 lists the details of sample spread and schools—Round 1 and Round 2). Eight hundred and four students took part in Round 2 with 791 usable responses. This data was gathered by the team from November 2002 to February 2003.

Data analyses

B-School impact has been assessed using the same sample T-tests on mean data gathered at Round 1 and Round 2.

Table 1.2   **Super league schools—sample details (usable and complete formats)**

S.No.	Institute	Round—1	Percentage	Round—2	Percentage
1.	Bajaj	104	8.09	83	10.49
2.	IIMA	200	15.55	93	11.76
3.	IIMB	182	14.15	74	9.36
4.	IIMC	135	10.50	75	9.48
5.	IIML	167	12.99	115	14.54
6.	MDI	135	10.50	115	14.54
7.	S. P. Jain	132	10.26	83	10.49
8.	XIMB	114	8.86	56	7.08
9.	XLRI	117	9.10	97	12.26
	Total	1286	100.00	791	100.00

Notes: See Appendix 1a and 1b in Chapter 4 of this book for profile write ups of each school which participated in the study.

Part 2: Perceptions of the corporate sector (corporate executives and alumni)

One of the roles of the B-School is to meet the requirements of corporate sector, since they are the key employers of management graduates. Therefore, data was gathered from the corporate world to identify their perceptions regarding the competencies which students bring to the corporate world after their MBA programmes. The following have been assessed in this work:

1. Corporate (corporate executives) perspectives on:

   (a) Needed managerial competencies in the business context,
   (b) Perceived managerial competencies in the business context, and
   (c) Competencies needed in the future

2. Alumni perspective on:

   (a) Needed managerial competencies in the work context,
   (b) Managerial competencies acquired in the B-School,
   (c) Beliefs and values at entry and exit levels (self rating by alumni), and
   (d) Perceived importance of competencies contributing to career growth.

Self report questionnaires were developed by interviewing academicians and corporate sector executives to assess both corporate perspective as well as alumni perspective (see Appendices 4, 5, and 6 for the details).

APPENDICES

Appendix 1: Self assessed competency— definitions

Definitions of the attributes[1], are presented here:

Managing Self has been assessed by using the six attributes presented below:

1. **Emotional Self Awareness**—The degree to which one is able to notice feelings, label them, and connect to their source.
2. **Emotional Awareness of others**—The ability to hear, sense, or intuit what other people may be feeling, from their words, body language, and other cues.
3. **Intentionality**—Ability to act deliberately, to say what you mean and mean what you say. It involves managing distractions, awareness of deeply felt motivations and consistently working to make things happen.
4. **Positive Outlook**—Extent to which you view the world and your place it, in an optimistic or pessimistic sense.
5. **Compassion**—Ability to be exceptionally empathetic, to appreciate, and honour another person's feelings and point of view. Compassion also consists of your ability to forgive yourself and others.
6. **Resilience**—Ability to bounce back, retain a sense of curiosity and hopefulness about the future, even in the face of adversity.

Influencing others has been assessed by using the four attributes presented below:

1. **Emotional Expression**—The ability to verbalize your emotions in a way that puts this information to productive use.

2. **Interpersonal Connections**—Ability to create and sustain a network of people with whom you are your real and whole self; to whom you can express caring and appreciation; with whom you can share your vulnerabilities and hopes.

3. **Constructive Discontent**—The ability to stay calm, focused and emotionally grounded, even in the face of disagreement or conflict.

4. **Trust Radius**—The degree to which you expect people to be trustworthy, to treat you fairly, to be inherently good.

Managing Complexity has been assessed by the two attributes below:

1. Intuition—The ability to use non-cognitive cues to navigate through potentially overwhelming or conflicting information, derive important insights or sense opportunities.

2. Creativity—Ability to tap multiple, non cognitive resources that allow you to envision powerful new ideas, frame alternative solutions and find effective, new ways of doing things.

Managing Diversity has been assessed by the two attributes below:

1. Flexibility[2]—has been operationalized as the characteristic of being open to new experiences, liking change and variety, and being patient. High score indicates person who likes change, variety, easily bored by routine life and everyday experiences, impatient, and even erratic. A low score indicates the opposite—not prone to change, likes a steady pace and well organized life, may be stubborn, even rigid.

2. Tolerance—Intolerance of ambiguity[3] has been defined as the 'way people look at and respond to unclear and vague situations, in a threatening manner, leading to avoidance of

the situation'. Higher the score, greater the intolerance of ambiguity; the lower the score, greater the ambiguity tolerance.

Appendix 2: Psychometric instruments used for self assessment—scale reliability

Establishing validity and reliability of scales is an important requirement in any research work. Statistical analysis enables this. Alpha tests were conducted to assess scale reliability. The alpha values of the scales (see below) range from 0.61 to 0.81[4]. Hence, the reliability of all the instruments in the Indian context on a student sample stands established.

Alpha values of the psychometric scales

Scales	Items	Alpha value
Emotional Self Awareness	6	0.6860
Emotional Expression	8	0.7146
Emotional Awareness of Others	11	0.7623
Intentionality	13	0.7126
Creativity	10	0.7395
Resilience	12	0.7532
Interpersonal Connections	7	0.6937
Constructive Discontent	8	0.6129
Positive Outlook	8	0.8141
Compassion	9	0.6518
Intuition	9	0.7581
Trust Radius	10	0.6983
Flexibility	21	0.7354
Tolerance—Intolerance of Ambiguity	14	0.7528

Appendix 3: Psychometric self assessment—competency clusters (statistical basis)

Factor analysis of the scales used in the study

Principal component analysis has been done on all the scales together to enable the regrouping of tests for development of the four dimensions—managing self, influencing others, managing complexity, and managing diversity. The factor loadings indicate the absence of multi co-linearity except in the case of four attributes—personal power, radical orientation, dependency, and tolerance, which loaded on more than one factor and hence were subsequently dropped.

Appendix 4: Measurement of stakeholders views—perceptions of corporate executives

Questionnaire development

The questionnaire was initially prepared by the research team and discussed with five experts from academia. This was followed by a focused group discussion with two groups (five members each group) of senior corporate executives. The questionnaire contains both structured as well as unstructured questions.

Sampling and data collection

Initially, 650 large companies in India were sent questionnaires addressed to the CEO. Since the response was zero, senior persons (from the top 50 large recruiting companies as well as some other well known organizations recruiting business school graduates

Combined factor analysis of the 18 scales—rotated component matrix

	1 Managing self	2 Influencing others	3 Managing diversity	4 Managing complexity
Emotional Self Awareness	.541			
Emotional Expression		.613		
Emotional Awareness of Others	.599			
Intentionality	.712			
Creativity				.701
Resilience	.729			
Interpersonal Connections		.659		
Constructive Discontent		.687		
Positive Outlook	.658			
Compassion	.564			
Intuition				.620
Trust Radius		.665		
Personal Power	.574	.523		

Flexibility		.659	
Tolerance–Intolerance of Ambiguity		-.844	.501
Radical*		.487	
Dependency*	-.578	-.510	
Tolerance*	.550	.396	

Notes: (SPSS package) Per cent of Variance Explained (cumulative – 57.67); Extraction Method: Principal Component Analysis; Rotation Method: Varimax with Kaiser Normalization(converged in 11iterations) n = 1350; Only factors with eigen value 1 and above are retained.

* Scales dropped from analysis owing to loading or more than one factor (indicating co-linearity)

from top schools) were contacted by the researchers. Thus the method of sampling has been purposive, focusing on getting a wide representation across industry segments as well as getting responses of very senior persons in the industry, with extensive experience working with graduates of top schools.

We could interact and get data from 107 persons from 80 organizations, primarily in the multinational and Indian private sector segment, since they are the largest recruiters of MBAs from the top schools. Data was collected using the interview method, while, structured questionnaire were personally filled up by the interviewees themselves.

The participants of the study were predominantly male, engineers with MBA degrees, aged 30 years and above. The sample consisted predominantly of HR professionals with a strong top level representation, with more than 10 years of work experience. They represent a wide and representative range of industry segments, from manufacturing to consulting.

Background information regarding the Sample

Area of expertise (N=90)	Frequency	Percentage
HR	72	80.00
Other	18	20.00

Appendix 5: Measurement of stakeholders views: Alumni perceptions-questionnaire, sampling and data collection

Questionnaire development consisted of a two-stage method:

(a)   Discussion with experts and

(b) Focused group discussions with 10 alumni of two business schools.

The questionnaire for this section, consisted of questions regarding beliefs (entry stage and exit stage), competencies mastered through B-School education, suggestions regarding competencies to be inculcated for the future; skills needed to manage growth and performance challenges in the initial stages and the extent to which B-School inputs helped in dealing with these challenges. Data was collected using the self report questionnaire (structured and unstructured) mailed to 500 alumni of various schools. Three hundred and thirty four usable questionnaires were received—a 66.80 response rate.

The sample consisted of 334 alumni across nine schools which participated in the study—45 per cent (22–25 yrs age); 55 per cent (26–36 yrs age); majority (80 per cent) were male; 67 per cent were engineers. Majority of the sample (79 per cent) had 1–2 years of work experience, while the rest had three years and above work experience.

Appendix 6: Alumni perceptions-definitions and competency classification

Seventeen skills and competency dimensions were identified through an expert group discussion. Recruiters were asked to rate their perceptions regarding business school graduates as a group on a five-point scale. Given below is the broad categorization along with the definitions:

1. **Task Management related Competencies**

   (a) Thinking on your feet—Ability to come up with quick solutions.
   (b) Prioritization—Ability to organize tasks at hand in terms of relevance and importance as per time deadlines.
   (c) Performance Focus—Ability to focus energy on delivering the results.
   (d) Problem Solving—Focus on finding solutions.
   (e) Communication and Presentation Skills—Powerful articulation ability and capability to convey through multiple media.
   (f) Analytical Ability—Apply logical linear thinking and deduce.
   (g) Dealing with Ambiguous Situation/Tolerance of Ambiguity—Ability to function optimally in a poorly structured fuzzy context/fluid situation.
   (h) Flexibility—Ability to shift one's mindset/stance in response to the changing scenario.
   (i) Global Mindset—Capacity to think in a global context.
   (j) Risk Taking—Ability to step beyond the conventional mode and try something different, which can be beneficial to the organization.

2. **People Management**

   (a) Leadership Skills—Capacity to influence the thinking of relevant people in one's own work sphere.
   (b) Interpersonal Skills—Capacity to initiate, establish relationship, interact.
   (c) Negotiation Skills—Capacity to convince, present views, data and facts cogently and get the best outcomes in a given situation.

    (d) Diversity and Conflict Management Skills—Capacity to listen, accommodate, and tolerate contrary viewpoints and also defuse deadlocks between people and within groups.

    (e) Team Working—Ability to work with other team members.

3. **Maturity**

    (a) Self Confidence—A positive self evaluation which leads to a capacity to step beyond the conventional/an ability to take challenges and meet them.

    (b) Ability to sustain Work Pressure—Ability to stretch beyond the normal according to the business requirements.

APPENDIX NOTES

1. Attributes under Managing Self, Influencing Others and Managing Complexity have been measured using some of the scales developed by Esther Orioli (2000) based on the work done by Cooper and Sawaf (1997).
2. Flexibility scale from the California Psychological Inventory (Gough 1987).
3. Composite scale (Singh and Bhandarker 1996, 1994, and Nalini 1999).
4. .60 alpha value has been used in the literature as the minimally acceptable cut off point for retaining items in a test. Hence, those items where the alpha value did not reach .60 were dropped.

NOTES

1. The importance of higher education continues to grow in an age of technology-driven innovation and change. The report of the task force on higher education in developing countries (IBRD, The World Bank 2000) concluded that tomorrow's world will demand highly qualified specialists and increasingly specialized generalists, clearly emphasizing the importance of higher education.
2. The Goldman and Sachs report (1999) projected that India has the most rapid growth potential among the BRIC countries (Brazil, Russia, India, and China). The report however suggests that India will have to take drastic steps to develop relevant skills.

REFERENCES

Abramson, L. Y., M. E. P Seligman, and J. D. Teasdale., 1978. 'Learned helplessness in humans: Critique and reformulation', *Journal of Abnormal Psychology*, 87: 49–74.

Agor, W. A., 1986. 'The logic of intuition: How top executives make important decisions', *Organizational Dynamics*, 14(3): 5–18.

Akhtar, S. and A. Singh., 1972. 'Value system approach for motivation', Executive Motivation in N.K. Singh (1982). *Current Concerns, foundation for organizational research.* New Delhi.

Allinson, C. W., E. Chell, and J. Hayes., 2000. 'Intuition and Entrepreneurial Behaviour', *European Journal of Work and Organizational Psychology*, 9: 31–43.

Amabile, T. M., 1997. 'Motivating creativity in organizations: On doing what you love and loving what you do', *California Management Review*, 40(1): 39.

Amundson, N., 1995. 'An interactive model of career decision making', *Journal of Employment Counselling*, 32: 11–21.

Andersen, J. A., 2000. 'Intuition in Managers: Are intuitive managers more effective?', *Journal of Managerial Psychology*, 15(1): 46.

Argyris, C., 1976. *Increasing Leadership Effectiveness*. New York: John Wiley.

Ashford, S. J., and A. S. Tsui., 1991. 'Self regulation for managerial effectiveness: The role of active feedback seeking', *Academy of Managerial Journal*, 34: 251–280.

Aspen study., 2002. 'Where will they lead us: MBA attitudes towards business and society.' <http://www.aspen.org>

Atwater, L. E., and F. J. Yammarino., 1992. 'Does self other agreement on Leadership perceptions moderate the validity of leadership and performance predictions?', *Personal Psychology*, 45: 141–64.

Avolio, B. J., 1999. *Full Leadership Development: Building the Vital Forces in Organizations*. Thousand Oaks: SAGE.

Barbuto, Jr., E. J., and M. E. Burbach., 2006. 'The Emotional Intelligence of Transformational Leaders: A Field Study of Elected Officials', *Journal of Social Psychology*, 146(1): 51–64.

Barnevik, P., cited in Taylor, W. E., 1991. 'The logic of global business: an interview with ABB's Percy Barnevik', *Harvard Business Review*, 69(2): 93–105.

Bar-On, R., 1997. *The Emotional Quotient Inventory (EQ-I): Technical and Manual*. Toronto: Multi Health Systems.

———., 2000. 'Emotional and Social Intelligence: Insights from the EQ Inventory', in R. Bar-On and J. D. A. Parker (eds), *The Handbook of Emotional Intelligence-Theory of Development, Assessment and Application at Home, School and in the Workplace*. San Francisco: Jossey-Bass.

Barron, F., 1969. *Creative person and creative process.* New York: Holt, Reinhardt Winston.

Bartlett, C. A., and S. Ghoshal., 1992. 'What is a global manager?' *Harvard Business Review*, 70: 124–132.

Bass, B. M., 1985. *Leadership and Performance Beyond Expectations.* New York: Free Press.

Baumgartel, H. J., 1986. 'MBA Development Study: An Overview of Findings and Conclusions', *Management and Labour Studies*, 11(4): 201–219.

Beglerp, T. M., and D. P. Boyd., 1986. 'Psychological charactersistics associated with entrepreneurial performance.' Paper presented at the Babson Entrepreneurship Research Conference, Welseley, MA.

Behling, O., and H. Eckel, 1991. 'Making sense out of intuition', *Academy of Management Executive*, 5: 46–54.

Bennett, R.H. 1998. 'The importance of tacit knowledge in strategic deliberations and decisions', *Management Decision*, 36: 589–597

Bennis, W., 1997. *Why Leaders Can't Lead: The Unconscious Conspiracy Continues.* USA: Jossey-Bass.

Bennis, W., and B. Nanus., 1985. *Leaders: The Strategies for Taking Charge.* New York: Harper and Row.

Bennis, W., and J. O. Toole., 2006. 'How business schools lost their way', *Harvard Business Review*, 83(5): 96–104.

Bentz, V. J., 1985. 'A view from the top: A thirty year perspective of research devoted to the discovery, description, and prediction of executive behaviour.' Paper presented at the 93rd Annual Convention of the American Psychological Association, LosAngeles.

Bernardin, H., 1986. 'Subordinate appraisal: a valuable source of information about managers', *Human Resource Management*, 25: 421–39.

Bharuch and Leeming., 1996. 'Programming the MBA programme: The quest for curriculum', *Journal of Management Development*, 15(7): 27–36.

Blake, R. R., and J. S. Mouton., 1964. *The Managerial Grid*. Houston: Gulf Publishing.

Boal, K. B., and C. J. Whitehead., 1992. 'Cognitive and behavioural complexity and flexibility', in R. L. Phillips, and J. G. Hunt, (eds), *Strategic Leadership: A Multiorganizational-Level Perspective*. Westport, CT: Quorum, pp. 237–55.

Bolin, L. A., 1997. 'Entrepreneurial leadership: New paradigm research discovering the common characteristics and traits of entrepreneurs who have served successfully in leadership position.' Unpublished dissertation, Walden University.

Bossidy, L., and R. Charan., 2002. *Execution: The Discipline of Getting Things Done.* New York: Crow and Business Publishing.

Bowers, D. G., and S. E. Seashore., 1996. 'Predicting Organizational Effectiveness with a Four Factor Theory of Leadership', *Administrative Science Quarterly*, 4: 238–63

Boyatzis, R. E., 1982. *The Competent Manager.* New York, NY: John Wiley and Sons.

———., 1996. 'Competencies can be developed, but not in the way we thought', *Capability*, 2(2): 25–41.

Boyatzis, R. E., D. Goleman, and K. Rhee., 2000. 'Clustering Competencies in Emotional Intelligence—Insights from the Emotional Competencies Inventory', in Ruven Bar-On, and J. D. A. Parker (eds), *The handbook of Emotional Intelligence: theory Development, assessment, and application at home, school, and in the workplace.* San Francisco: Jossey-Bass, pp. 343–362.

Boyatzis, R. E., A. McKee, and D. Goleman., 2002. 'Reawakening your passion for work', *Harvard Business Review*, pp. 86–96.

Brake, T., 1997. *The Global Leader. Critical Factors for Creating the World Class Organization.* Chicago, IL: Irwin Professional Publishing.

Budner, S., 1962. 'Intolerance of ambiguity as a personality variable', *Journal of Personality*, 30(1): 29–59.

Burke, L. A., and M. K. Miller., 1999. 'Taking the mystery of intuitive decision making', *The Academy of Management Executive*, 13(4): 91

Burke, W., E. Richley, and L. DeAngelis., 1985. 'Changing leadership and planning processes at the Lewis Research Centre, National Aeronautics and Space Administration', *Human Resource Management*, 24: 81–90.

Burns, J. M., 2003. *Transforming leadership: A new pursuit of happiness.* NY: Atlantic Monthly Press.

Chang, E. C., ed., 2001. *Optimism and Pessimism: Implications for Theory, Research and Practice.* Washington, DC: American Psychological Association.

Chen, C., 1998. 'Understanding career development: A convergence of perspectives', *Journal of Vocational Education and Training*, 50(3): 437–61.

Chin, R., and B. Kenneth., 1984. 'General Strategies for Effecting Change in Human Systems', in W. Bennis, R. Chin, and K. D. Benne (eds), *The Planning of Change.* New York: Holt, Reinhart and Winston.

Church, A., 1997. 'Managerial Self Awareness in high performing individuals in organizations', *Journal of Applied Psychology*, 10(1): 3–34.

Church, A., and J. Waclawski., 1999. 'Influence behaviours and managerial effectiveness in lateral relations', *Human Resource Development Quarterly*, 10(1): 3–34.

Coleman, J. S., 1988. 'Social Capital in the Creation of Human Capital', *American Journal of Sociology*, 94: S95–S120.

Conger, J. A., 1989. *The Charismatic Leadership*. San Francisco: Jossey-Bass.

Conger, J. A., and R. N. Kanungo. eds, 1988. *Charismatic Leadership: The Elusive Factor in Organizational Effectiveness*. San Francisco: Jossey-Bass, pp. 213–236.

Cooper, R. K., and A. Sawaf, 1997. *Executive EQ: Emotional Intelligence in Business*. London: Orion Business Books.

Corr, P. J., and J. A. Gray., 1996. 'Attributional style as a personality factor in insurance sales performance in the UK', *Journal of Occupational and Organizational Psychology*, 69: 83–87.

Covin, J. G., D. P. Slevin, and M. B. Heeley., 2001. 'Strategic decision making in an intuitive vs. technocratic mode: Structural and environmental considerations', *Journal of Business Research*, 52: 51–67.

Crossan, M. M., H. W. Lane, and R. E. White., 1999. 'An organizational learning framework: From intuition to institution', *Academy of Management Review*, 24: 522–537.

Dane, E., and M. G. Pratt., 2007. 'Exploring Intuition and Its Role in Managerial Decision Making', *Academy of Management Review*, 32(1): 33–54.

Dayal, I., 2001. Report and Recommendations of the committee on policy-perspectives for management education, Ministry of HRD (Government of India), April.

Deutschman, A., 1991. 'The Trouble with the MBAs', *Fortune*, 124(3): 67–77.

Doyle, K., 1992. 'Mastering Motivation', *Incentive*, 166(3): 20–23.

Druskat, U., and S. B. Wolff., 2001. 'Group emotional intelligence and its influence on group effectiveness', in C. Cherniss and

D. Goleman (eds), *The Emotional Intelligent Workplace.* Jossey-Bass, pp. 132–155

Entrialgo, M., E. Fernandez, and C. J. Vázquez., 2000. 'Characteristics of Managers as Determinants of Entrepreneurial Orientation: Some Spanish Evidence', *Enterprise and Innovation Management Studies*, 1(2): 187–205.

Eroglu, S., and B. K. Pilling., 1994. 'An Empirical Examination of the Impact of Salesperson Empathy and Professionalism and Merchandise Salability on Retail Buyers' Evaluations', *Journal of Personal Selling and Sales Management*, 14(1): 45–58.

Fiedler, F. E., 1967. *A theory of leadership effectiveness.* New York: McGraw-Hill.

Frank Report. 1963. Cited in Colin Tabot., 1997. 'Paradoxes of management development—trends and tensions', *Career Development International*, 2(3): 119–146.

Gardner, H., 1999. *Intelligence Reframed: Multiple Intelligences for the 21st Century.* New York: Basic Books.

Gillham, J., ed., 2000. *The Science of Optimism and Hope.* Radnor, PA: Templeton Foundation Press.

Goldman Sachs., 1999. 'Goldman and Sachs Report'. Accessed from http://www2.goldmansachs.com/our-firm/investors/financial/acheived/annual-reports/attachments/1999-annual-report.pdf.

Goleman, D., 1998. *Working with emotional intelligence.* New York: Bantam Books.

———., 2000. 'Leadership that gets results', *Harvard Business Review*, 78(2): 78–92.

Gordon, A. G. and J. E. Howell., 1959. *Higher Education for Business.* New York: Columbia University Press.

Gough., 1987. *Manual for the California Psychological Inventory.* California, Palo Alto: Consulting Psychologists Press.

Gowing, M., 2001. 'Measurement of individual emotional competence', in C. Cherniss and D. Goleman (eds), *The Emotional Intelligent Workplace*. Jossey-Bass, pp. 83–131.

Greenleaf, R. K., 1977. *Servant leadership: A journey into the nature of legitimate power and greatness*. New York: Paulist Press.

Gregersen, H. B., A. J. Morrison, and J. S. Black., 1998. 'Developing Leaders for the Global Frontier', *Sloan Management Review*, 40(1): 21–32.

Gupta, A., and Govindarajan., 2002. 'Cultivating a global mindset', *Academy of Management Executive*, 16(1): 116–126.

Handy, C., 1988. *Making Managers*. London: Pitman.

Heames, J., and R. W. Service., 2003. 'Dichotomies in Teaching, application and ethics', *Journal of Education for Business*, 79(2): 118–122.

Hersey, P., and K. H. Blanchard., 1977. *The Management of Organizational Behaviour* (3rd Ed.). Engelwood Cliffs, NJ: Prentice-Hall.

Hisrich, R. D., and A. D. Jankowicz., 1990. 'Intuition in venture capital decisions: An exploratory study using a new technique', *Journal of Business Venturing*, 5: 49–62.

Hogan, R. T., G. J. Curphy, and J. Hogan., 1994. 'What Do We Know about Personality, Leadership and Effectiveness', *American Psychologist*, 49: 493–504.

Hogarth, R. M., 2001. *Educating intuition*. Chicago: University of Chicago Press.

House, R. J., 1973. 'A path-goal theory of leadership effectiveness', in E. A. Fleishman and J. G. Hunt (eds), *Current Developments in the Study of Leadership*. Carbondale, IL: Southern Illinois University Press, pp. 321–328.

———., 1977. 'A 1976 theory of charismatic leadership', in J. G. Hunt and L. L. Larson (eds), *Leadership: The Cutting*

Edge. Carbondale, IL: Southern Illinois University Press, pp. 189–207.

———., 1996. 'Path-goal theory of leadership: Lessons, legacy, and a reformulated theory', *Leadership Quarterly*, 7: 323–52.

Humphreys, R. H., 2002. 'The Many Faces of Emotional Leadership', *The Leadership Quarterly*, 13(5): 493–504.

IBRD., 2000. 'Higher Education in Developing Countries—Peril and Promise'. http://siteresources.worldbank.org/EDUCATION/ resources/2782001099079877269/547664-1099079956815/ peril_promise_en.pdf, last accessed on 27th June 2008.

Jacobson, R. L., 1993. 'Shaking up the MBAs, The Chronicle of Higher Education', *Journal of Applied Psychology*, 82: 281–292.

Jones, G. R., and J. M. George., 1998. 'The Experience and Evolution of Trust: Implications for Cooperation and Teamwork', *Academy of Management Review*, 23(3): 531–546.

Kehman and Barclay., 1969, in G. Lindzey, and E. Aranson (eds), *The Handbook of Social Psychology* (2nd Ed). New Delhi: Amerind Pub. Co.

Kellett, J., R. H. Humphrey, and R. G. Sleeth., 2002. 'Empathy and complex task performance: two routes to leadership', *The Leadership Quarterly*, 13: 523–544.

Kelley, R., 1998. *How to be a star at work*. New York: Times Books.

Kets de Vries, M. F., and C. Mead., 1992. 'The development of the global leader within the multinational corporation', in V. Pucik, N. M. Tichy, and C. K. Barnett (eds), *Globalizing management: Creating and leading the competitive organization*. New York: John Wiley and Sons, pp. 187–205.

Khatri, N., and H. A. Ng., 2000. 'The role of intuition in strategic decision making', *Human Relations*, 53(1): 57.

Kirton, M. J., 1976. 'Adaptors and innovators: A description of a measure', *Journal of Applied Psychology*, 61(5): 622–629.

———., 1981. 'A reanalysis of two scales of tolerance of ambiguity', *Journal of Personal Assessment*, 45(5): 407.

Koen., C., and S. Crow., 1995. 'Human relations and political skills', *HR Focus*, 50(2): 19.

Koh, H. C., 1996. 'Testing hypotheses of entrepreneurial characteristics: A study of Hong Kong MBA students', *Journal of Managerial Psychology*, 11(3): 12–25.

Kotter, J., 1999. *What Leaders Really Do*. Harvard Business School Press.

Kouzes, J. M., and B. Z. Posner., 1995. *The Leadership Challenge: How to Keep Getting Extraordinary Things Done in Organizations* (2nd Ed). San Francisco: Jossey-Bass.

Krishnan, V., 2003 'Do business schools change students' values along desirable lines?' in S. M. Natale, and Libertella (eds), *Business Education and Training: A Value Laden Process*. Vol 8: 26–39, University Press of America, Lanham, Maryland and Oxford University Centre for the Study of Values in Education and Business.

Lank, A., and E. Lank., 1995. 'Legitimizing the gut feel: The rise of intuition in business', *Journal of Management Psychology*, 10(5)–23.

Loevinger, J., 1976. *Ego Development*. San Francisco: Jossey-Bass.

Maddi, S. R., and S. C. Kobasa., 1984. *The Hardy Executive: Health under Stress*. Homewood, IL: Dow Jones-Irwin.

Martin, C. D., 1996. 'The involuntary push: University mergers and their effect on post-graduate management education in South Australia', *Journal of Educational Administration*, 34(3): 83–91.

McAllister, D. J., 1995. 'Affect and cognition based trust as foundations for interpersonal cooperation in organizations', *Academy of Management Journal*, 38(1): 24–59.

McCall, M. W., Jr., M. M. Lomabardo, and A. M. Morrison., 1988. *Lessons of Experience*. Lexington, MA: Lexington.

McCall, Morgan., 1998. High Flyers: *Developing Next Generation Leaders*. Harvard Business School.

McClelland, D. C., 1973. 'Testing for Competence rather than Intelligence', *American Psychologist*, 28.1: 1–40.

McFadzean, E. S., 1998. 'Enhancing creative thinking within organizations', *Management Decision*, 36(5): 309–15.

McGregor, D., 1966. *Leadership and Motivation*. Cambridge, MA: MIT Press.

Merriam-Webster's Online Dictionary., 2005. Retrieved April 30, 2005, from Merriam-Webster's Online database, http://www.m-w.com.

Mintzberg, H. and Joseph Lampel., 2001. 'Do MBAs Make Better CEOs', *Fortune*, February 19.

Mishra, M., 1995. 'Intolerance of Ambiguity and Rigidity', *Indian Journal of Psychology*, 70(142): 29–33.

Mitchell R., P. N. Friga., and Ronald K. Mitchell., 2005. 'Untangling the Intuition Mess: Intuition as a construct in entrepreneurship research', *Entrepreneurship Theory and Practice*, 29(6): 653–79.

Moran, R. T., and J. R. Reisenberger., 1994. *The Global Challenge: Building the New Worldwide Enterprise*. London: McGraw-Hill Book Company.

Nalini, T. P., 1999. *Cultural Ethos: Its Impact on Managerial Values and Styles*. Doctoral Thesis Submitted to Osmania University.

Orioli, E., K. H. Trocki, and T. Jones., 2000. *EQ Map Technical Manual*. San Francisco: Essi Systems, Inc.

Pescolido, A. T., 2002. 'Emergent leaders as managers of group emotion', *The Leadership Quarterly*, 13(5): 583–599.

Peterson, C., 1988. 'Explanatory Style as a risk factor for illness', *Cognitive Therapy and Research*, 12(2): 117–130.

Philip, J., 1992. 'Management Education in India: Past, Present and Future', *Vikalpa*, 17(4): 19–24.

Pierson, F. C., 1959. *The Education of American Businessman*. New York: McGraw-Hill.

Pinard, M., and R. J. Allio., 2005. 'Innovations in the Classroom: Improving the creativity of MBA Students', *Strategy and Leadership*, 33(1): 495–51.

Porter, L. W., and L. E. McKibbin., 1988. *Management Education and Development*. New York: McGraw Hill Book Company.

Prahalad, C. K., and G. Hamel., 1990. 'The Core Competencies of the corporation', *Harvard Business Review*, 68(3): 79–91.

Prince, C., and J. Stewart., 2000. 'The dynamics of the corporate education market and the role of business schools', *The Journal of Management Development*, 19.3: 207–219.

Proudfoot, J. G., P. J. Corr, D. E. Guest, and J. A. Gray., 2001. 'The development of a scale to measure occupational attributional style in the financial services sector', *Personality and Individual Differences*, 30(2): 259–270.

Rhinesmith, S. H., 1996. *A Manager's Guide to Globalization. Six Skills for Success in a Changing World*. New York: McGraw-Hill.

Rosen, R., and P. Brown., 1996. *Leading People: Transforming Business from the Inside Out*. New York: Viking.

Rosen, R., P. Digh, M. Singer, and C. Philips., 2000. *Global literacies: Lessons on Business Leadership and National Cultures*. New York: Simon and Schuster.

Roth, W. 1990. 'Keeping the jungle out of MBA classrooms', *Personnel*, 67(9): 4–6.

Roy, M., and S. Dugal.,1998. 'Developing trust: the importance of cognitive flexibility and co-operative contexts', *Management Decision*, 36(9): 561–67.

Satia, J. K., 1992. 'Reshaping Management Education', *Vikalpa*, 17(4): 25–27.

Schein, E. H., 1992. *Organization Culture and Leadership* (2nd Edition). San Francisco: Jossey-Bass.

Schere, J., 1982. 'Tolerance of ambiguity as a discriminating variable between entrepreneurs and managers.' Paper presented at the Academy of Management Annual Meeting.

Schneider, M., 2002. Business Week Online.11 March. (http://www.businessweek.com/bschools/content/mar2002/bs2002038_0311.html)

Schulman, P., 1995. 'Explanatory style and achievement in school and work', in G. Buchanan and M. E. P. Seligman (eds), *Explanatory Style*. Hillsdale, NJ: Lawrence Erlbaum, pp. 159–171.

———., 1999. 'Applying learned optimism to increase sales productivity', *Journal of Personal Selling and Sales Management*, 19(1): 31–37.

Segal, M., 1997. *Points of Influence: A Guide to Using Personality Theory at Work*. San Francisco: Jossey-Bass.

Selen, W., 2001. 'Learning in the new business school setting: a collaborative model', *The Learning Organization*, 8(3): 106–113.

Seligman, M. E. P., 1990. *Learned optimism: How to change your mind and your life*. New York: Pocket Books.

Seligman, M. E. P., and P. Schulman., 1986. 'Explanatory Style as a predictor of productivity and quitting among life insurance sales agents', *Journal of Personality and Social Psychology*, 50(4): 832–838.

Sexton and Bowman (1984) cited by Schiebe, F and Dex, S., 1998. in 'Should we have more family friendly working policies?', *European Management Journal*, 16(5): 586–599.

Sheridan, J. H., 1993. 'A New Breed of MBA', *Industry Week*, 242(19): 11–16.

Sheth, N. R., 1992. 'Some Thoughts on Management Education', *Vikalpa*, 17(4): 29–32.

Shipper, F., and J. E. Dillard., 1994. 'Comparing the managerial skills of early derailers vs. fast trackers, late derailers vs. long-term fast trackers, and mid-career derailers vs. recoverers.' Paper presented at the meeting of the Academy of Management, Dallas, TX.

Simon, H. A., 1987. 'Making management decisions: The role of intuition and emotion', *Academy of Management Executive*, 1: 57–64.

Singh, P., and A. Bhandarker., 1990. *Corporate Success and Transformational Leadership*. New Delhi: Wiley Eastern.

———., 1994. *IAS Profile: Myth and realities*. New Delhi: Wiley Eastern.

———., 2002. *Winning The Corporate Olympiad—The Renaissance Paradigm*. New Delhi: Vikas Publishing House Pvt. Ltd.

Singh, P., A. Bhandarker, and L. Prasad., 1996. 'Paradigm shifts in the Indian Industry: The need for tolerance of ambiguity', *MDI Management Journal*, 9(2).

Singh, P., A. K. Jain, and A. Bhandarker., 2006. 'Meaning of work in corporate India- Preliminary findings', in P. Singh, A. Bhandarker, and J. Bhatnagar (eds), *Future of work-mastering change*. New Delhi: Excel Books, pp. 63–73.

Sosik, J. J., and L. E. Megerian., 1999 Understanding Leader Emotional Intelligence and Performance. *Group and Organization Management*, 24(3): 367–390.

Spencer, L. M. Jr., and S. M. Spencer., 1993. *Competence at work: Models for superior performance.* New York: John Wiley and Sons.

Spreitzer, G. M., and R. E. Quinn., 1996. 'Empowering middle managers to be transformational leaders', *Journal of Applied Behavioral Science*, 32(3): 237–261.

Spreitzer, G. M., M. McCall, and J. D. Mahoney., 1997. 'Early Identification of International Executive Potential?', *Journal of Applied Psychology*, 82(1): 6–29.

Srinivas, K. M., 1995. 'Globalization of the Business and the Third World: Challenge of Expanding the Mindset', *Journal of Management Development*, 14(3): 26–49.

Stogdill, R. M., and B. M. Bass., 1981. *Stogdill's handbook of leadership: A survey of theory and research* (Revised and expanded/edition). New York: Free Press.

Stoltz, P., 1996. *AQ Performance Studies.* California: PEAK Learning, Inc.

———., 2000. *Adversity Quotient at work: Finding your hidden capacity for getting things done.* New York: HarperCollins Publishers Inc.

Sylvester, J., F. Patterson, and E. Ferguson., 2003. 'Comparing two attributional models of job performance in retail sales: A field study', *Journal of Occupational and Organizational Psychology*, 76(1): 115–118.

Tichy, N., and M. A. Devanna., 1986. *The Transformational Leader.* USA: John Wiley and Sons.

Tornow, W. W., 1993. 'Perceptions or reality: is multiple-perspective measurement a means or an end?', *Human Resource*

Management, 32. *Traits of entrepreneurs who have served successfully in leadership positions.* Unpublished Dissertation, Walden University. Westport, CT: Quorum

Van Velsor, E., S. Taylor, and J. Leslie., 1993. 'An examination of the relationships among self-perception accuracy, self awareness, gender and leader effectiveness', *Human Resource Management*, 32(2): 249–63.

Wolff, S. B., A. T. Pescolido, and V. U. Druskat., 2002. 'Emotional intelligence as the basis of leadership emergence in self managing teams', *Leadership Quarterly*, 13.

Yammarino, F. J., and B. M. Bass., 1990. 'Long-Term forecasting of transformational leadership and its effects among naval officers', in K. E. Clark (ed.), *Measures of Leadership*. West Orange, NJ: Leadership Library of America.

Yukl, G., 1997. 'Effective leadership behaviour: A new taxonomy and model.' Paper presented at the Eastern Academy of Management International Conference, Dublin, Ireland.

Zacker, J., 1973. 'Authoritarian avoidance of ambiguity', *Psychological Reports*, pp. 901–902.

Zaleznik, Abraham., 1977. 'Managers and Leaders: Are they Different?', *Harvard Business Review*, 55(3): 67–78

Chapter 2
The MBA graduate-perceptions of Corporate India

'Begin with the end in mind'—this famous adage is true for all organizations and institutions engaged in the business of creating products and services for end-users-customers. **Customerization** is therefore the key mantra for building excellence, not only in products but also in processes, systems, and strategies. It is this approach which helps organizations to stay continuously relevant and responsive to customer requirements and thereby enables them to grow, succeed, and win.

In reality, this oft repeated mantra is—however—not adequately practiced by many institutions since they do not have robust systems of getting continuous feedback about the product-customer match. In order to be close to the customers and stay relevant to them, it is therefore essential to continuously seek feedback about the product and services rendered by the institutions.

This mantra is equally true for B-Schools, since they are in the business of grooming and shaping talent for the business world—the end user. In order to stay continuously relevant, B-Schools must therefore get feedback from the end users—the corporate world. It is equally important that B-Schools gather information from their own alumni—how they perceive the relevance and utility of their grooming in the corporate context and their expectations from B-Schools.

It is in this perspective that the present chapter has been organized.

Part 1 of this chapter examines the perceptions of the Corporate Executives while Part 2 focuses on the perceptions of the Alumni.

PART 1—B-SCHOOL GRADUATES IN THE EYE OF THE CORPORATE EXECUTIVES[1]

Part 1 has four sections:

- Section A delineates the Skills and Competencies of B-School graduates—Desired vs. Actual,
- Section B maps out the Needed Future Competencies,
- Section C highlights Workplace Adjustment Issues, and
- Section D examines the Personality Related Concerns.

(A) MANAGERIAL SKILLS AND COMPETENCIES-DESIRED

Desired managerial competencies from B-School graduates

Table 2.1 presents the perceptions of senior level executives[2] recruiting graduates of top B-Schools in India. Analyses of the table indicates that the competencies are in four broad clusters. The statements in the first cluster have percentages 78.89 and above, the second cluster has responses ranging from 50–55.56 per cent, the third cluster has percentages ranging from 24.44–44.44 per cent and the fourth cluster has percentages below 24.44.

The first cluster consists of five competencies—team working, performance focus, leadership skills, analytical power, self confidence (ranked from 1 to 5—the percentages ranging from 78.89 per cent to 94.44 per cent). The second cluster comprises of four competencies—risk taking, ability to sustain work pressure, flexibility, and interpersonal skills (ranked 6–9 respectively, percentages from 55.56–50 per cent). The third cluster constitutes of two competencies—ability to prioritize and ambiguity tolerance (ranked 10 and 11, the percentages ranging from 44.44 per cent to 24.44 per cent).

Table 2.1 Top B-School graduates: desired competencies

Competencies	Frequency N = 90	Percentage	Rank
Ability to Work in a Team	85	94.44	1
Performance Focus	80	88.89	2
Leadership Skills	79	87.78	3
Analytical Ability	75	83.34	4
Self Confidence	71	78.89	5
Risk Taking	52	55.56	6
Capability to Sustain Work Pressure	48	53.33	7.5
Flexibility	48	53.33	7.5
Interpersonal Skills	45	50.00	9
Ability to Prioritize	40	44.44	10
Dealing with Ambiguous Situation	22	24.44	11
Global Mindset	15	16.67	12
Problem Solving	11	12.22	13
Managing Diversity and Conflict	10	11.11	14.5
Communication and Presentation Skills	10	11.11	14.5
Thinking on One's Feet	07	07.78	16
Negotiation Skills	03	03.33	17

Note: Responses will not total 100 per cent since respondents had to select 7 most important out of 17 items.

The last cluster comprises of six competencies—global mindset, problem solving, managing diversity and conflict, communication, thinking on your feet and negotiation skills (the ranks ranging from 11 to 17, percentages ranging 24.44 per cent and below).

Table 2.2 presents the actual competencies demonstrated by the graduates. There are three clusters of competencies discernable in this table. The first cluster has percentages ranging from 78 per cent and above; the second cluster has percentages ranging from 24.44–33.33; while the third cluster has percentages below 16.67.

Table 2.2   **Top B-School graduates—perceived managerial competencies**

Perceived competencies	Frequency N = 90	Percentage	Rank
Analytical Ability	90	100.00	2
Self Confidence	90	100.00	2
Communication and Presentation Skills	90	100.00	2
Capability to Sustain Work Pressure	88	97.78	4
Thinking on One's Feet	71	78.88	5
Negotiation Skills	30	33.33	6
Risk Taking	26	28.89	7
Performance Focus	22	24.44	8.5
Global Mindset	22	24.44	8.5
Interpersonal Skills	15	16.67	10.5
Leadership Skills	15	16.67	10.5
Ability to Prioritize	14	15.56	12
Managing Diversity and Conflict	13	14.44	13.5

(*Continued*)

(*Continued*)

Perceived competencies	Frequency N = 90	Percentage	Rank
Dealing with Ambiguous Situation	13	14.44	13.5
Problem Solving	11	12.22	15
Flexibility	10	11.11	16.5
Ability to Work in a Team	10	11.11	16.5

Note: Responses will not total 100 per cent since respondents had to select 7 most important out of 17 items.

The first cluster has five competencies—analytical power, self confidence, and communication skills (100 per cent each) at rank 1, followed by capacity to withstand work pressure at rank 4 (97.78) and the capacity to (make decisions and) solve problems at rank 5 (78.88). The second cluster consists of four competencies—negotiation skills, risk taking, performance focus, and global mindset (ranked 6th, 7th, 8.5, 8.5 respectively, the percentages ranging from 24.44–33.33). A small percentage of the sample (1/6th and below) perceive the graduates demonstrating Interpersonal competencies (rank 10.5), Leadership skills (rank 10.5), managing diversity and conflict (rank 13.5), and ability to work in a team (rank 16.5). These findings reveal that people-centric skills which form the core of leadership are poorly inculcated in B-School graduates.

Gap analyses: Desired vs. actual competencies

Table 2.3 presents the comparative picture of the desired vs. actual competencies. Analysis of this table indicates that the two lists are significantly different from each other, the Rho value of 0.06 being insignificant at $p = >0.01$ levels. In other words, there is a significant mismatch between the graduates being groomed by the top B-Schools and the competencies required by the business world.

Table 2.3 **Desired vs perceived competencies of B-School graduates**

	Desired N = 90			Actual N = 90		
	Freq.	*Percentage*	*Rank*	*Freq.*	*Percentage*	*Rank*
Ability to Work in a Team	85	94.44	1	10	11.11	16.5
Performance Focus	80	88.89	2	22	24.44	8.5
Leadership Skills	79	87.78	3	15	16.67	10.5
Analytical Ability	75	83.33	4	90	100.00	2
Self Confidence	71	78.89	5	90	100.00	2
Risk Taking	52	55.56	6	26	28.89	7

(Continued)

(*Continued*)

	Desired N = 90			Actual N = 90		
	Freq.	Percentage	Rank	Freq.	Percentage	Rank
Ability to Sustain Work Pressure	48	53.33	7.5	88	97.78	4
Flexibility	48	53.33	7.5	10	11.11	16.5
Interpersonal Skills	45	50.00	9	15	16.67	10.5
Ability to Prioritize	40	44.44	10	14	15.56	12
Dealing with Ambiguous Situation/ Ambiguity Tolerance	22	24.44	11	13	14.44	13.5
Global Mindset	15	16.67	12	22	24.44	8.5
Problem Solving	11	12.22	13	11	12.22	15
Managing Diversity and Conflict	10	11.11	14.5	13	14.44	13.5
Communication and Presentation Skills	10	11.11	14.5	90	100.00	2
Thinking on your Feet	7	7.78	16	71	78.88	5
Negotiation Skills	3	3.33	17	30	33.33	6

Note: Rho = 0.06– Not Significant at p > 0.01 level. To be significant rho has to reach the table value of .62 (table 25, Garrett 1985: 373).

The aforementioned analysis brings out that B-School graduates are not adequately groomed on 11 of the 17 listed competencies, as indicated by the poor response percentages—below 33.33 per cent. As mentioned earlier, this list includes people-management competencies like interpersonal skills, leadership skills and ability to work in a team, which was however rated as extremely important by corporate executives. In the eyes of the corporate executives, execution-related competencies in this list—risk taking; performance focus, ability to prioritize, and flexibility—have also featured quite low. However, it is heartening to note that corporate executives have a positive view about B-School grooming on Analytical ability, self confidence, communication and presentation skills, capability to sustain work pressure, and thinking on one's feet.

Some of the commonly held opinions and views[3] of the corporate executives about the perceived competencies of B-School graduates are presented below. The quotes have been cited to convey the intensity of the concerns as well as the spirit articulated by the corporate executives in the interview. In fact, in many cases, the quotes speak louder than the numbers.

Poor People Skills of B-School Graduates: The poor ranks on People Skills like interpersonal skills, team working and leadership in the above table are further supported through the following quotes. Majority (80 per cent) of the interviewed executives felt strongly about the inadequate people-related skills among the graduates. Some of the key views are cited below:

- 'They are individualists and often prefer working alone' (30)
- 'Do not know how to work with people'(23)
- 'Poor on EQ' (7)
- 'They are highly competitive and want all credit for themselves, therefore find it difficult to influence people' (16)
- 'They have poor Inter Personal Skills' (22)
- 'Do not know how to relate with peers and subordinates' (14)
- 'Arrogant and condescending attitude' (5)

The view on the importance of people related competencies has been beautifully summed in the following quote:

'[Managers] need an incredible degree of collective working and cross-functional leveraging; H.R and people management domains are the weakest in business school education; this should be rectified since these factors are highly relevant in the context of performance' (1)

These quotes indicate that the individualistic approach of the graduates makes it difficult for them to network with people especially peers and subordinates. They do not realize the importance of 'managing people', 'influencing others', and 'creating impact' and in the absence of people-related competencies, their ability to mobilize, influence and persuade other relevant colleagues becomes quite constrained.

Inadequate Execution Mindset: A large percentage (75) of the sample mentioned poor execution orientation. The views have been cited below:

- 'They have a 'consultant' orientation' (24)
- They do not want to 'dirty their hands' (35)
- 'They are too impatient and unwilling to go through the grind' (19)
- 'They are poor implementers (50)

Some of the key suggestions for developing execution mindset are cited below:

- *'They need to know the drivers behind success and failure; [B-Schools need to] teach them about performance and implementation; 'Today knowledge is a commodity and freely available. What we are lacking are skills of execution and performance. At least, initiate work on this in the business school' (12)*

- *'More emphasis on execution is needed to groom them better for the real world' (15)*
- *'Delivery competencies will have to be inculcated in the students so that they can become productive on the job as soon as possible' (11)*
- *'They must think strategically, must make things happen, convert thoughts into action' (9)*
- *'They must hit the ground running' (18)*
- *'We look at management graduates for greater productivity. Can they put theories into practice?' (5)*

These quotes, powerfully, bring out the need for cultivation of the execution mindset among the graduates.

Cognitive capabilities for cultivating Entrepreneurial Orientation: Three attributes which contribute to entrepreneurial orientation—ambiguity tolerance (rank 13.5), business sense (15), and flexibility (16.5)—also feature low in the list. Some of the views on thinking styles and cognitive capabilities of the graduates are given next:

- *'They are too linear in their approach' (21)*
- *'As long as things are well defined they are able to deliver; when things become uncertain they become uneasy and find it difficult to perform' (25)*
- *'They feel comfortable to work in a predictable world and want everything to be mapped out and*

clear. Frankly today's world is so uncertain that no company can talk about their plans beyond a couple years' (30)

- *'Business school syllabus produces needless rigidity and prepares students to operate in a predictable world' (5)*

The following quotes indicate the needed cognitive capabilities:

- *'Creative thinking will become increasingly essential' (50)*
- *'They should be taught the capacity to thinking systematically as well as out of the box, and bring fresh perspective to understand a given problem' (15)*
- *'They should learn to get away from the tyranny of the BOOK—they are unable to understand the contextual sensitivity and respond to it; they look for pat solutions from the books' (1)*

(B) FUTURE COMPETENCY REQUIREMENTS: (CORPORATE PERCEPTIONS)

The famous saying goes, 'Prepare today for tomorrow'. Those who do not think of their tomorrow will spoil both, their today as well as their tomorrow. Thus, to groom business leaders of tomorrow, B-Schools need to develop requisite competencies not merely for the present but also for the emerging future. It is in this perspective that executives were asked to peep into the future and share their views about emerging shifts in competencies.

As shown in Table 2.4, 81.08 per cent of the sample feels that the emerging business scenario will be different from the present and therefore the required competencies will also witness a change.

Table 2.4 **Perceived need for change in competency requirements**

Change in competency requirements in future	Frequency N = 74	Percentage
Yes	60	81.08
No Change	14	18.92

Some of the quotes presented in the following list describe the likely future direction and the velocity of change which is likely to besiege the corporate world.

- 'Future will be increasingly chaotic' (31)
- 'Chaos will become the rule of the game' (20)
- 'Lightening speed of response will decide the winner' (12)

- *'Business-ship of tomorrow will experience thunder-storms above and turbulent waters below' (1)*
- *'Future belongs to those who can shape the complexity' (11)*
- *'Leaders of tomorrow must develop the sense of finding opportunities in the problems' (6)*
- *'In the future only the paranoid will survive' (5)*
- *'In the future even the humble Maruti 800 can dent the grand Merc' (1)*

Table 2.5 indicates that leading change has emerged as the most important future competency requirement (rank 1—81.08), followed by entrepreneurial and risk taking abilities (rank 2—76.68), developing global mindset (rank 3—60.81) and ambiguity tolerance (rank 4—50)

Table 2.5   **Future competency requirements (corporate perceptions)**

	Sample *N = 74*	*Percentage*
Leading Change	60	81.08
Entrepreneurial Abilities	56	76.68
Developing Global Mindset	45	60.81
Ambiguity Tolerance	37	50.00

Note: Quantification from content analysis of open ended questions, responses will not tally 100.

Leading change

Leading change featuring at number 1 is understandable especially given the change imperative faced by organizations. The dynamic speed of changes in the business context creates a state of flux and fluidity where nothing is certain and predictable. As phenomena of this kind gather greater momentum, organizations and executives will need to cope with ambiguity and thrive. According to the interviewed executives from Telecom, FMCG, Hospitality and Textiles, change has become a constant in their organizations—for example short cycles of restructuring exercises, faster change in business cycles, coping and thriving in contexts of change and adversity which create ambiguity, requires different kinds of mindsets, attitudes and thought processes, suggesting shift in needed competencies.

Entrepreneurial orientation and ambiguity tolerance

Increasing competition has rendered the business context volatile and full of flux and this necessitates managerial ability to thrive in such a scenario. Corporate executives in the study mentioned that attributes like need for commercial/business perspective (35), speed, high drive, high achievement-orientation, result focused (55), practical orientation and terrific execution skills (49), assertiveness and self starter type of personalities (28) are important and will be increasingly needed by future leaders. Future leaders will have to achieve and execute at great pace based on incomplete information and deliver results in half the time (16)

B-School graduates will also need to develop and use intuitive capabilities:

- *'In the future with emergence of greater turbulence managers will need to use their intuition (along with analytical abilities) to make decisions' (11)*
- *In the future, 'Young managers will need to cultivate an entrepreneurial mindset, one who can mobilize their people, who can seize opportunity and create wealth—such managers will be tomorrow's outstanding business leaders—who can take risks, make quick decisions' (1)*
- *'To enable them to work in today's dynamic contexts, we need to teach them how to create the rules, question assumptions and challenge them; today nothing is set and therefore experimenting, exploring and comfort with change are needed. How to teach them through the business school curriculum this is the challenge' (12)*
- *'The typical linear and analytical framework which students imbibe in business schools will not be*

adequate to thrive in such an environment. In the future, business school graduates will need the ability to ask questions, assess and size up the problem, conceptualize it and frame it. This will become especially important for us as companies go up the business value chain' (16)

- *'They need the ability to deliver in situations characterized by fluidity and flux' (6)*

Globalization-related competencies

Corporate executives whom we interviewed also emphasized that in the future developing Global mindset will be the new frontier:

- *'Need to understand how common markets work; impact of the currency fluctuations on business, forex, and common currency' (18)*

- *'Awareness of competition laws; what constitutes violation of international law should be emphasized' (15)*

- *'Working globally implies the need to build ethical awareness and orientation, since international laws have become very tough now' (21)*

These views reflect the need for developing greater global awareness (according to the corporate sample) regarding the socio-economic, political-legal imperatives of successfully working in the global context.

These four future competency requirements clearly indicate that the future will need a different kind of manager, someone comfortable in change contexts, entrepreneurial in orientation, curious and excited by ambiguity, and with ability to operate on a global stage. Comparison of the desired profile, according to the corporate executives, with the thrust of B-School education indicates that there is a significant gap since B-Schools do not adequately focus on building the desired managerial competencies.

(C) WORKPLACE ADJUSTMENT ISSUES

Table 2.6 presents a discomfiting picture about the top B-School graduates. Perusal of this table indicates that B-Schools have failed to inculcate pragmatic wisdom among the graduates. It is extremely disheartening to note that around 85 per cent executives feel that B-School graduates have poor reality orientation, followed by high personal ambition, and great hurry to reach the top—80 per cent. They are perceived as arrogant rank 3–73.33); having unrealistic expectations (rank 4–48.57) and prefer only glamorous jobs (rank 5–30.48).

Table 2.6 **Mindset and attitudes of top B-School graduates**

	Frequency N = 105	Percentage	Rank
Poor Reality Orientation	89	84.76	1
High (personal) Ambition-want to Reach Top in a Hurry	84	80.00	2
Arrogant/Chip on the Shoulder	77	73.33	3
Unrealistic CEO Mindset	51	48.57	4
Glamorous' Job	32	30.48	5
Poor Learning Orientation	27	25.71	6
Condescending Approach	23	21.90	7
Unhealthy Peer Comparisons	10	9.52	8

Note: Open ended question; responses have been quantified through content analyses; percentages will not total to 100 since multiple responses have been given.

It is also disappointing to notice their poor learning orientation (rank 6), condescending approach (rank 7), and unhealthy peer comparisons, the percentages ranging from 48.57 to 9.52.

To get in-depth insights into the psyche of the top B-School graduates, some of the quotes are presented below spanning across the dimensions cited in the table above:

Poor reality orientation

- *'Their general knowledge is poor — I have had people tell me in selection interviews ' we do not have the time to read newspapers!' (42)*
- *'They prefer cozy desk jobs. They are good at research, sitting in the office and creating models etc.' (13)*
- *'They have poor appreciation of ground realities and seem insensitive to the context' (15)*

Poor knowledge of ground realities means that graduates come to work with inordinately high expectations. Most of the respondents (85 per cent) mentioned expectations management of the graduates as one of the key challenges being faced at the induction stage: 'They expect the moon from their jobs; students come into corporate sector with high expectations. The ground realities of corporate life come to them as a big shock and they start their work life on a negative note. The media hype on salaries has further accentuated this phenomenon. Many corporate executives are seriously considering going only for laterals (people with work experience) to top B-Schools for their manpower needs.

Preparing graduates for corporate realities, dealing with their arrogant attitude, and basically shaping certain values and attitudes—learning orientation, realistic planning for own career, are some of the challenges which need to be addressed at least partly by B-Schools, so that graduates transition into the work place and adjust smoothly.

High personal ambition

Eighty per cent of the respondents have mentioned *'High ambitions and desire to reach the top in a hurry'* as an attitudinal problem. This has been also expressed as follows:

- *'They believe that they are born to be on the top',* *(60)*
- *'They want to occupy top positions as soon as possible.' (56)*

While ambition is positive, the desire to reach the top 'in a hurry' is viewed as the concern area. The following quote beautifully illustrates the impact of such unbridled self-focused ambition, 'Youngsters come in with high personal ambitions. Nothing wrong with it because it fuels growth, but over the years it (the ambition) is getting negative—their interest lies only in what is in it for themselves. We need people with positive ambition, with desire to contribute to the team' (1).

In the quest for growth, graduates seem to be missing the point about the importance of learning and the passion to contribute—

'Few graduates seem to have passion for the subject or for the industry; there is low curiosity and drive to do something. This is not very healthy for growth of industry. B-School graduates think that business success is more about managing money and markets and making swank presentations. Their learning curve is gone. Their concept of growth is designation, not contribution- unlike the technologist. He further elucidates-Owing to the passion for the subject and desire to contribute, somewhere the technologist stands tall as compared to the management graduate' (1)

Unfortunately, salary seems to be the most important factor on a person's mind when he goes for placement interviews.

'Students focus on salaries and do not bother with job quality, opportunity for better exposure when they pick up a job ...' (41)

A telling comment has been made by a global CEO:

'I have not seen a single outstanding business graduate from the top schools in the last 7 years. Depth of subject knowledge, passion, curiosity and therefore learning orientation are missing' (1)

Arrogance and chip on the shoulder

Most of the sample (73.33) has indicated that graduates from business schools carry a 'chip on the shoulder'. They have an 'arrived attitude' as if to say they have proved their worth by landing a seat in a top business school. This attitude has been described as:

- *'They think that they are God's gift to the corporate world' (Director HR—Indian MNC)*
- *'They expect the same status and importance on the job as they get socially (as an MBA). They look for differential treatment' (VP-HR, Indian Conglomerate)*
- *'They think they are "the cream" but unfortunately they are unable to relate with all, unable to admit mistakes and also unfortunately, unable to provide leadership'(Group President—Indian Conglomerate)*

This leads to 'arrogance while dealing with others' and 'inability to admit to having made a mistake', as well as 'inability to ask for help'. They are over-confident, have no doubts, rarely seek clarifications, and work as per their own thinking. This appears to be one of the biggest blocks and as such learning orientation and issue focused approach of the graduates is affected.

'Unrealistic CEO mindset'

This attribute has been mentioned by 48.57 per cent of the sample. Inadequate appreciation of key success factors and low concern about the 'nitty-gritty' issues go along with this are some of the other concerns. Many of the interviewed executives expressed the view that graduates somehow carried the mindset that while they themselves are here to do the big stuff like strategy, others are supposed to deal with the details and make things happen.

- *'All of them want to do strategy...They speak the language of strategy but do not put energy into the details' (23)*
- *'They do not realize that unless they convert ideas into results, ideas are of no use. Today ideas are available in plenty, the challenge lies in converting them into results' (29)*

As the head HR of an Indian conglomerate put it:

'Success depends 'not on ideas, but on converting ideas into action'. When faced with routine tasks, graduates feel that their talents are not being appreciated and put to good use. They feel that the job is 'not exciting'; 'there is no learning taking place'. The above reveals that work expectations of graduates, especially those who

are fresh out of college seem to be overly romanticized and tend to lead to disappointment.

'Glamorous job' is also a disquieting finding. It is fashionable among business schools to 'look for the glamorous jobs—marketing and finance. In fact graduates, who are put into less glamorous jobs, wait to leave and join a more glamorous job when they get the opportunity. This has consequences for the corporate sector—for example the biggest crisis is in HR, quality, and manufacturing where few good people are available at the entry stages. The challenges of paradigm shift of organizations on these parameters thus remain inadequately attended to.

This also impacts at the individual level—those without great aptitude for marketing or finance end up in such jobs, owing to high peer pressure on the campuses. The rest who ultimately end up getting into the so-called 'unglamorous' jobs are unhappy and perform indifferently, biding their time to leave.

Close-mindedness and Poor Learning orientation reflects another unproductive attitude of the graduates of top business schools. 'They hate to admit it when they do not know something, they dislike having to acknowledge making a mistake. They do not realize they cannot bullshit their way to the top in the age of 360 degree feed back'.

'**Condescending attitude to other business schools graduates**' and '**Batch hierarchy**' have also been mentioned. Management graduates take it for granted that their growth should have a faster pace relative to others with or without delivering results. This has been expressed as follows:

- *'They consider themselves to be superior to the graduates of other business schools. They experience severe crises when they get left behind while their batch-mates have been promoted. They should realize that the good old days when such things were still possible in large companies are over. Today, only performance talks. The business school one comes from is only the entry passport, not the golden chute which will carry them up without outstanding results' (Director-FMCG).*

- *'They must realize today's work reality. In banks, back-end jobs are mostly outsourced. Management trainees want to do product development jobs, which they can only if they have an appreciation of customer requirements. Doing a front-end job (developing general management skills) for a while is essential' (Dir HR Multinational Bank).*

- *'They should realize that 60 per cent of business revenue comes from retail—most of them want to do product management or credit; they do not want to pitch for sales or operations' (VP HR, Infotech).*

Although an accelerated pace of career growth is possible depending on one's performance, these statements make it amply clear that there are no short cuts. The unrealistic mindsets and over-inflated ego are perhaps an outcome of lack of work experience, ignorance about the corporate world as well as the sense of achievement of having made it to a top B-School. Unless a change in attitude takes place, unfortunately there is a high chance of career derailment. The MBA is an entry passport to a good career, not a lifetime guarantee. By the time they accept the need to learn, change, and work with people, it may be too late for them to do anything about it. How to deal with this attitude problem is the big challenge both for the B-School and the industry.

(D) GRADUATES PERSONALITY PROFILE: CORPORATE PERCEPTIONS

B-School graduates have been perceived to have poorly developed personality and interest profiles according to majority of the sample (55). Observation by practitioners especially from global companies has highlighted issues regarding the profile of Indian students:

- *'Our people do very well abroad but they are very narrowly focused, do not have broad range of interests.*

Our managers should be more connected to the real world—art, music, etc—to enable them to develop more complete personalities' (11)

- 'Indians are selected for our global pool because they are so bright, but beyond analytical skills, they do not stand out as leaders, in comparison to the others. They are unable to move beyond a level up the (hierarchy) for this reason' (5)

- 'They focus too much on developing analytical skills but beyond a point this does not help them. By the time they realize this 7–8 yrs down the line, its too late' (11)

- 'Our recruitees are very bright, but do not have a broad perspective; in fact they are quite uni-dimensional; in the first year or two after they join, we cant take them even for client meetings—they have no other interests, nothing to talk about, unable to make small talk, keep a conversation going…these are essential skills' (3)

- *Indeed all globalizing Indian companies will increasingly face such a need, and will have to shape their own people, in order to smoothen the wheels of interpersonal relationship and strike immediate rapport while interacting globally (1)*

- 'Problems regarding the angular personality development is not because of business schools alone. However, business schools should acknowledge this problem and try to do something about this. Nor can business schools develop leaders through a course, *but we can get them thinking on their strengths and weaknesses, so that they can take the responsibility for their own development' (3)*

This section clearly brings out the need to develop all round personality of graduates. Future success of Indian MBAs on the global stage will depend not only on strong analytical abilities but on development of overall personality so that they can operate with greater maturity and ability to cultivate and relate with others.

PART II—B-SCHOOL GRADUATES: EYE OF THE ALUMNI[4]

Findings in Part II have been presented in three sections:

i. Managerial Skills and Competencies of the Graduates,
ii. Career Success Centric Competencies, and
iii. Beliefs and Values of the Alumni.

(A) Managerial skills and competencies[5]

This section examines—(*i*) the self perceived skills and competencies (mastered); (*ii*) The competencies to be inculcated (suggested); and (*iii*) The comparison between the mastered and suggested competencies.

i. Skills and Competencies mastered in the MBA program—Self perceived

Table 2.7 presents the overall responses on the skills and competencies mastered during the MBA programme. Three broad categories based upon the intensity of response have emerged in the table. The first category has percentages ranging from 60.20–70.10; the second category ranging from 43.70–57.20, and the third category scores being 48.50 and below.

The first category comprises three competencies—*communication and presentation skills* (rank 1–70.10), followed by *analytical ability* (rank 2–63.20), and *self-confidence* (rank 3–60.20). The second group consists of five competencies—*problem-solving skills* (rank 4–57.20), followed by *performance focus* (rank 5–55.70), *interpersonal skills* (rank 6–54.20), *thinking on one's feet* (rank 7–53.90), and *dealing with ambiguous situation* (rank 8–50). The third and last cluster includes nine competencies—*global mindset* (rank 9–48.50), *ability to prioritize* (rank 10–43.70), *risk taking* (rank 11–42.30), *leadership skills* (rank 12–39.20), *flexibility* (rank 13–38.30), *capability to work under pressure* (rank 14–37.40), *ability to work in a team* (rank 15.5–32), *managing diversity and conflict* (rank 15.5–32), and *negotiation skills* (rank 17).

Table 2.7 Skills and competencies: mastered versus suggested

Skills and competencies (self-perceived)	Mastered			Suggested		
	Frequency	Percentage	Rank	Frequency	Percentage	Rank
Communication and Presentation Skills	234	70.10	1	174	52.10	8
Analytical Ability	211	63.20	2	135	40.40	12
Self Confidence	201	60.20	3	140	42.90	10
Problem Solving	191	57.20	4	115	34.40	15
Performance Focus	186	55.70	5	202	60.50	1.5
Interpersonal Skills	181	54.20	6	190	56.90	5
Thinking on Ones' Feet	180	53.90	7	191	57.20	4
Dealing with Ambiguous Situations	167	50.00	8	189	56.60	6
Global Mindset	162	48.50	9	202	60.50	1.5
Ability to Prioritize	148	42.30	10	133	39.80	13
Risk Taking	146	43.70	11	116	34.70	14
Leadership skills	131	39.20	12	177	53.00	7

(Continued)

(Continued)

Skills and competencies (self-perceived)	Mastered			Suggested		
	Frequency	Percentage	Rank	Frequency	Percentage	Rank
Flexibility	128	38.30	13	109	32.60	16
Capability to Sustain Work Pressure	125	37.40	14	102	30.50	17
Ability to Work in a Team	107	32.00	15.5	141	42.20	9
Managing Diversity and Conflict	107	32.00	15.5	137	41.00	11
Negotiation skills	106	31.70	17	194	58.10	3

Notes: N = 334; Rho = .32, not significant at p = >.01.

Perusal of this table indicates that people-centric competencies like *leadership skills, ability to work in a team, negotiation skills, and diversity and conflict management skills* have been inadequately developed in the B-School as indicated by the poor response percentages (below 39). Execution-related competencies like *ability to prioritize*, entrepreneurial competencies like *risk taking, flexibility, thinking on your feet*; as well as *global mindset* also feature in the category of competencies which are perceived to be poorly inculcated by the B-Schools (see the low ranks in cluster 3).

ii. Suggested Managerial Skills and Competencies to be inculcated by B-Schools

Table 5 deals with the views of alumni regarding skills and competencies to be inculcated by the B-Schools. Analysis of this table indicates that *global mindset as well as performance focus* competencies occupy the top most priority (60.50 each) *followed by negotiation skills* (58.10), and *thinking on your feet* (57.20). Further analysis of this table indicates that *interpersonal skills* (56.90), *dealing with ambiguous situation* (56.60) *leadership skills* (–53), and *communication and presentation skills* (–52.10) are moderately rated their ranks being 5, 6, 7, and 8 respectively.

iii. Skills and Competencies—Alumni View: Mastered vs. Suggested

A comparative picture of the Mastered vs. Suggested lists indicates that there is a significant difference between the two sets of ranks as reflected by the insignificant 'Rho' value. The low-rated competencies in the mastered list—*Performance focus, Global mindset, Negotiation skills, and Thinking on your feet*—emerge high in the suggested list, indicating that they are the most critical competencies to be inculcated in the B-School. However, their poor ranking (1.5, 1.5, 3 and 4) indicates that B-Schools have not adequately focused on inculcating these competencies.

(B) Career success centric competencies

Human beings demonstrate intense aspiration to succeed and perform. This is more so in the MBA graduates who bring high aspirations and ambition to grow, succeed and perform[6]. It is in this per-spective that needed competencies for career success—career growth and performance have been examined.

Table 2.8 presents the analysis of the performance centric as well as career growth-related competencies. A glance at the table shows that *Delivering timely results* has been rated at the top of both the competency

Table 2.8 Career–success–centric competencies—career growth and performance

Managerial challenges	Career growth related			Performance related		
	Frequency	Percentage	Rank	Frequency	Percentage	Rank
Managing Superior	198	59.30	1	145	43.40	2
Delivering Timely Results	146	43.70	2	186	55.70	1
Leading Team	122	36.50	3	125	37.40	4
Motivating People	104	31.10	4	134	40.10	3
Managing Conflicts	96	28.70	5	114	34.10	5
Managing Customers	87	26.00	6	94	28.10	7
Managing Colleagues	73	21.90	7	107	32.00	6
Managing Subordinates	48	14.40	8	69	20.70	8
Managing Competitors	47	14.10	9	36	10.80	9
Managing Dealers	14	04.20	10	21	6.30	10
Managing Distributors	08	02.40	11	18	5.40	11

Note: N = 334; rho 0.97 sig. at p = > 0.01 level.

lists—performance as well as growth—(that is rank 1 and rank 2). Further perusal of this table indicates that there are four top people-centric competencies important for career growth—*managing superior* (rank 1), *leading team* (3), *motivating people* (4), and *managing conflicts* (rank 5). These competencies also feature at the top on the performance-related competencies list, their ranks being 2, 4, 3, and 5 respectively. Both the lists are very similar to each other as indicated by the Rho value: 0.97 significant at $p = >0.01$ level.

Other competencies for both, performance and career growth are unfortunately not adequately developed in the B-School as is evident from Table 2.8.

Role of B-Schools in shaping graduates for career success

In this segment of the analysis an attempt has been made to examine the role played by B-Schools in shaping these competencies. Table 2.9 sharply brings out that on all the dimensions, the mean values are below 3, except *delivering timely results* (3.56). This indicates the success of management schools in inculcating speedy result orientation among B-School graduates. However, when we compare the needed competencies for success and performance as analyzed in table, B-Schools have miserably failed in building the top-rated competencies like team building, motivating people, and managing superior.

Table 2.9 **Competency development for career success**

Challenges	Mean	sd
Delivering Timely Results	3.56	1.82
Leading Team	2.96	1.83
Managing Conflicts	2.86	1.69
Managing Colleagues	2.77	1.70
Motivating People	2.75	1.79
Managing Customers	2.45	1.86
Managing Subordinates	2.12	1.73
Managing Superiors	2.08	1.73
Managing Competitors	2.01	1.92
Managing Dealers	1.48	1.71
Managing Distributors	1.30	1.64

Note: 5-point scale; (N = 334).

(C) Beliefs and values

Beliefs and values which one holds, powerfully influence one's attitudes and behaviour at work. In fact, psychologists consider them to be relatively permanent and deeply held desires of individuals, with powerful impact on attitudes and behaviour[7]. Table 2.10 presents the entry stage and exit stage beliefs and values of the alumni.

Table 2.10 Comparison of beliefs before joining B-School—after completing post-graduation

Beliefs and attitudes	Before-after comparison	Entry		Exit		t	Sig.
		m	sd	m	sd		
Integrity	*Erosion*	3.08	1.93	1.92	2.31	7.18	0.00
Achievement Orientation	*Improvement*	2.52	1.99	3.00	2.21	−2.65	0.01
People Orientation	*Improvement*	2.37	1.87	3.09	2.13	−4.76	0.00
Honesty	*Erosion*	2.34	2.21	0.52	1.44	13.66	0.00
Work Focus	*Improvement*	2.09	2.05	2.49	2.30	−2.48	0.01
Quality Orientation	*Improvement*	1.72	1.89	2.75	2.25	−6.16	0.00
Ideas and Concept Focus	*Improvement*	1.62	1.94	2.75	2.23	−6.97	0.00
High Time Orientation	*Improvement*	1.58	1.87	3.50	1.94	−13.120	0.00
Position and	*Improvement*	1.27	1.87	1.53	2.12	−1.84	0.07

Power Focus						
Religious Orientation	*Erosion*	1.19	1.83	0.35	1.08	7.97	0.00
Contribution Focus	*Improvement*	1.12	1.82	1.64	2.15	-3.56	0.00
Aesthetic Orientation	*Erosion*	1.05	1.76	0.74	1.84	3.16	0.00
Money and Material Things	*Improvement*	0.97	1.67	1.01	1.81	-0.48	0.63

Note: N = 334; 5 point scale; t values reaching .05 and above are considered to be significant.

Analysis of this table reveals that the top five beliefs and values held by alumni are Integrity followed by Achievement orientation, People orientation, Honesty, and Work focus, the mean values being 3.08, 2.52, 2.37, 2.34, and 2.09 respectively. Perusal of the table further brings out that Integrity is the only value which is moderately developed among the students before they enter the B-School, the mean being 3.08 on this dimension. Clearly, the other beliefs—achievement orientation, people orientation, honesty, work focus, quality orientation, ideas and concept focus, high time orientation, position and power focus, religious orientation, contribution focus, aesthetic orientation and money, and material things—have not been adequately developed prior to their entry into the programme as indicated by the below average mean scores (less than 3) on these dimensions.

In Table 2.10, the belief structure of the alumni has been presented. This has been done to assess the role played by B-Schools in shaping the belief systems of the students. These beliefs have been examined before entering the B-School and after passing out of the B-School. This has been done to assess the role played by B-Schools in shaping the belief system of the students. Analysis of this table indicates that B-School exposure has positively enhanced the intensity of beliefs held on nine dimensions, out of which there has been significant improvement in seven—achievement orientation, people orientation, work focus, quality orientation, ideas and concept focus, high time orientation and contribution focus. In the other two cases—position and power and money and material things—though there has been an improvement in the score, it is not statistically significant. Further analysis of this table brings out some disturbing findings, indicating significant value erosion on four beliefs/values—integrity, honesty, religious orientation and aesthetic orientation—from entry to exit stage.

The above findings indicate that while B-Schools have made a significant contribution in shaping work-centric values, they have however miserably failed in developing the spiritual component of the individual, which is the soul of the human being and the core of humanity. Similar findings have been reported by the some other studies (Aspen 2002; Krishnan 2003). The Aspen study (2002) brings out that graduates develop beliefs in maximizing shareholder value to the detriment of quality product, customer satisfaction, benefiting the environment, and community. Krishnan's study (2003) reveals that B-School experience has increased self centric values, and eroded societal centric values.

CONCLUSIONS

An attempt is made here to sketch the salient findings of this chapter. These findings are presented here in the context of the role of B-Schools in the eye of the corporate world as well as the alumni. In fact, this is the raison d'etre for the very existence of the B-Schools.

1. The corporate world has expressed positive views regarding the B-School graduates' competencies like analytical ability, self confidence, communication, and presentation skills and ability to sustain work pressure. Thus they feel that B-School graduates have powerful logical thought processes; they possess confidence in themselves, they are excellent communicators and they can cope with work pressures.

2. The corporate world, however, finds B-School graduates deficient on people-centric competencies like interpersonal skills, leadership, team work, and managing diversity and conflict. They feel the graduates are individualistic and solo players focused more on pursuing individual agenda rather than showing concern for teams and team goals. In this process of working with others, influencing, motivating, and leading others becomes a casualty. This is a matter of

concern because these qualities have been rated very high in the desired list of competencies by the recruiters.

3. The corporate world is concerned about their low flexibility, poor problem solving, inability to prioritize, incapability to deal with ambiguities and average performance orientation. In fact, they see B-School graduates more as advisors and consultants with little desire to dirty their hands. They are found to be impatient and poor in implementation. B-School graduates are seen to have low capability to deal with ambiguity and demonstrate low flexibility, which make them poor problem solvers. They are perceived to be linear, rigid and they do not know how to handle complex, uncertain, and ambiguous situations.

4. Corporate world perceives that to deal with the future business challenges effectively, B-School graduates must develop entrepreneurial orientation as well as capability to lead change, global mindset and ambiguity tolerance. Unfortunately on these dimensions, the corporate world does not view B-School graduates positively.

5. While expressing their views about the typical MBA mindset, the corporate sample highlights that MBAs from top schools are less pragmatic, highly ambitious, arrogant and carry unrealistic

CEO mindsets. They look for glamorous jobs and demonstrate poor learning orientation.

6. B-School alumni have assigned high priority to competencies like performance orientation, global mindset, negotiation skills, quick thinking, and interpersonal skills. They feel that B-Schools should pay greater attention to develop these skills and competencies among the graduates. However, they feel that these competencies are not adequately developed among B-School graduates during their MBA programme.

7. They express a positive view about the role played by B-Schools in developing communication capability and heightening linear and logical thinking among the graduates. They also feel B-School experience enables them to develop self confidence and problem-solving capabilities.

8. B-School alumni feel that their schools have failed in inculcating negotiation skills, ability to manage diversity, capability to work in a team, demonstrating flexibility and leadership skills along with taking risks, ability to prioritize and deal with ambiguity, and demonstrating global mindset.

9. Future business leaders (alumni) expressed positive views regarding the contribution made by

B-Schools in making them more achievement-oriented, people centric, developing higher quality consciousness, better work centric orientation and better focus on ideas and concepts. They also feel that B-School training helped them to develop greater time consciousness and in becoming more contribution focused.

10. Future business leaders also feel that during their training the criticality of integrity, honesty, religious, and aesthetic orientation, were not adequately emphasized.

11. In their perception, the emphasis (in the B-School) was more on developing work-related competencies to the detriment of societal-centric orientation.

12. B-School alumni demonstrate similarity in their perceptions about the competencies leading to career growth and performance in the organization. The feel that to grow and perform effectively, one needs to develop capability to manage superiors. They should be result centric; they should develop capability of working in teams and they should develop competencies to motivate and lead people. In their opinion B-Schools did not make significant contribution in developing these skills except building result-centric mindset.

NOTES

1. See Appendix 5, Chapter 1-for details of research methodology.
2. See Appendix 4, Chapter 1, pg 35 for sample details.
3. The in-depth interviews of 70 senior and top level corporate executives provided the material which was then analyzed and categorized.
4. Three hundred and sixty alumni across the nine schools–Bajaj, IIMA, IIMB, IIMC, IIML, MDI, SPJain, XLRI and XIMB—participated in this study. Data was collected using the self report questionnaire (structured and unstructured) mailed to 500 alumni of various schools. 334 usable questionnaires were received.
5. The speed, with which graduates adjust to work place demands and perform effectively, depends on their possessing many relevant managerial competencies. Understanding the role of B-School education in developing and shaping these competencies (from the alumni perspective in this case) is thus very relevant. The questionnaire used to gather corporate executives' perceptions (presented in Part 1 of this chapter), has also been used with the alumni.
6. Since most graduates join an MBA programme to enhance their career prospects, it was considered relevant to also examine the managerial competencies which they viewed as essential for career success. Career success has been measured using various criteria—better job, higher salaries, rapid pay increases, and rate of promotions. Findings on early career success of MBA graduates (O'Reilly and Chatman 1994), found it to be an outcome of general cognitive ability and motivation. Their findings brought out that those who were smarter and worked harder were more successful on measures like number of job offers, current salary, salary increments, and number of appointments.

7. Individual values are considered to be relatively stable and have a tremendous impact on attitudes and behaviour (Rokeach 1973, Meglino and Ravlin 1998, Krishnan 2003). Values have been found to impact work performance (see review in Claxton et al. 1996). There is evidence indicating that there is a good deal of instability in job values (Johnson 2001) during the transition from student to employee indicating that there is scope for development. There is evidence that the relative importance of values can be changed (Krishnan 2003, Rokeach 1973, Schwartz and Inbar-Saban 1988). Krishnan (2003) examined the value prioritization of graduates from a leading Indian B-School entry and exit stage. Findings on 229 students indicated that the prioritization of the four terminal values changed, becoming more self oriented and less other oriented. The Aspen study (2002) on values of graduates from across leading American business schools showed that there was change in value priorities after exposure to business school education—they gave greater priority to maximizing shareholder value and lesser priority to delivering high quality goods and services; social responsibility and environment were also low on the priority list.

REFERENCES

Aspen study., 2002. '*Where will they lead us: MBA attitudes towards business and society.*' <http://www.aspen.org>

Claxton, R. P., R. P. McIntyre, K. E. Clow, Jr., and J. E. Zamenak., 1996. 'Cognitive style as a potential antecedent to values', *Journal of Social Behavior and Personality*, 11(2): 355–73.

Garrett, H. E., and R. S. Woodworth., 1985. *Statistics in Psychology and Education* (Indian Reprint). Bombay: Vakil, Feffer, and Simon.

Johnson, M. K., 2001. 'Change in Job Values during transition to adulthood', *Work and Occupations*, 28(3): 315–345.

Krishnan, V., 2003. 'Do business schools change students' values along desirable lines?', in S. M. Natale and Libertella Volume 8 (eds), *Business Education and Training: A Value Laden Process.* (Immortal Longings), pp. 26–39. Lanham, Maryland: Uni-versity Press of America and Oxford University Centre for the Study of Values in Education and Business.

Meglino, B. M., and E. C. Ravlin., 1998. 'Individual values in organizations: Concepts, controversies, and research', *Journal of Management*, 24(3): 351–389.

O'Reilly, C. A. III, and J. A. Chatman., 1994. 'Working smarter and harder: A longitudinal study of managerial success', *Administrative Science Quarterly*, 39(4): 603.

Rokeach, M., 1973. *The Nature of Human Values.* New York: Free Press.

Schwartz, S. H., and N. Inbar-Saban., 1988. 'Value self—Confrontation as a method to aid in weight loss', *Journal of Personality and Social Psychology*, 54(3): 396–404.

Chapter 3

Impact of B-School education

World wide corporate leaders, accrediting institutions, management thinkers, and scholars have raised concerns and questions regarding the contributions made by B-Schools in shaping future business leaders. Such questions have been repeatedly expressed at various fora—corporate meets, meets organized by leading accreditation bodies—the European Quality Improvement System (EQUIS), the Association to Advance Collegiate School of Business (AACSB), the Association of MBA (AMBA), and NAB—as well as alumni get-togethers etc. The consensus emerging from these deliberations indicate the failure of B-Schools in developing effective managers and future business leaders.

It is in this perspective that the present chapter attempts to examine the impact of B-Schools in shaping future leaders. Impact analysis was carried out by calculating the significance of the difference between the two mean scores[1] on four of the leadership dimensions:

1. Self Management,
2. Influencing Others,
3. Managing Complexity, and
4. Managing Diversity

This chapter has been organized in four sections:

1. Section one deals with Managing Self dimension which includes six attributes:

    (a) emotional self awareness,
    (b) emotional awareness of others,
    (c) intentionality,
    (d) resilience,
    (e) positive outlook, and
    (f) compassion

2. Section two examines Influencing Others dimension comprising:

    (a) Emotional Expression,
    (b) Interpersonal connection,
    (c) Constructive discontent, and
    (d) Trust

3. Section three focuses on Managing Complexity which consists of:

    (a) Creativity, and
    (b) Intuition

4. Section four examines Managing Diversity consisting of Tolerance of Ambiguity and Flexibility, and

5. Section five presents the overall impact assessment across attributes assessed across the four sections.

1. MANAGING SELF: ACROSS SCHOOLS ANALYSIS

Through millennia, thinkers and philosophers have recurrently emphasized the criticality of managing self as an important competency to lead and influence others. This is in fact the most profound wisdom, since a human being has control—in a real sense—only on self. Unfortunately, one of the major crises of leadership occurs because people strive to manage others without exercising sufficient effort to manage self. Findings on six important attributes for self management:

(a) Emotional Self Awareness,
(b) Emotional Awareness of Others,
(c) Intentionality,
(d) Resilience,
(e) Positive Outlook, and
(f) Compassion

are examined hereafter.

Emotional self awareness (ESA)

Emotional Self Awareness consists of components like awareness of one's own feelings, recognizing them as well as understanding their root cause.

Examination of Table 3.1 indicates that graduates enter management schools with relatively high scores (all being in the Good Zone). This is true across all the nine schools[2]. Further analysis of this table brings out a positive shift in the scores from entry to exit stage in all the schools except Bajaj, IIML, and XIMB. In

Table 3.1 **Emotional self awareness: means, standard deviation, and T values**

B-Schools	Entry		Exit		t	Sig.
	m	sd	m	sd		
Bajaj	20.81	2.09	20.52	2.18	1.12	0.27
IIMA	19.84	2.49	19.98	2.55	−0.51	0.61
IIMB	20.25	2.58	20.32	2.50	−0.23	0.82
IIMC	20.31	2.20	20.45	2.08	−0.59	0.56
IIML	20.76	2.22	20.27	2.50	1.94	0.06
MDI	20.25	2.36	20.46	2.45	−0.96	0.34
S. P. Jain	20.68	2.42	21.28	1.99	−2.22	0.03
XIMB	20.67	1.99	20.15	2.40	1.54	0.13
XLRI	20.33	2.50	20.70	2.17	−1.77	0.08

Note: N = 791; Significance levels of 0.05 and above are considered adequate to indicate significant shift in mean values from entry to exit stage (indicating significant impact of the B-Schools).

these schools, the exit scores have slightly gone down. Perusal of this table reveals that although mean scores have improved in six schools—IIMA, IIMC, MDI, S. P. Jain, and XLRI—however, none of the means are significant except that of S. P. Jain (significant at p = >0.05 level).

Emotional awareness of others (EAO)

Emotional awareness of others reflects one's own ability to listen, sense or intuit the emotional state of others. In others words, it is the capability to recognize the feelings of others through their expression through words, body language, and other direct or indirect cues of behaviour.

Perusal of the emotional awareness of others scores (Table 3.2) indicates that graduates enter with 'very good' scores[3] and this is clearly evident in all the schools. This table indicates a positive shift in scores across all the schools. Further analysis indicates that out of nine schools, significant scores shifts have however taken place in the case of only four schools—Bajaj, IIMB, MDI, and XLRI. In the case of the rest—IIMA, IIML, IIM-C, S. P. Jain, and XIMB—though there have been positive shifts, they are however not significant at p ≥ 0.05 level.

Table 3.2 **Emotional awareness of others: means, standard deviation, and T values**

B-Schools	Entry		Exit		t	Sig.
	m	sd	m	sd		
Bajaj	32.33	3.69	34.21	4.40	−4.44	0.00
IIMA	31.35	4.11	31.58	4.42	−0.53	0.60
IIMB	31.60	4.47	33.14	4.89	−3.21	0.00
IIMC	32.32	3.86	33.02	4.46	−1.63	0.11
IIML	32.99	4.47	33.66	4.95	−1.63	0.11
MDI	32.28	4.43	33.68	4.91	−3.49	0.00
S. P. Jain	33.16	4.20	33.63	3.69	−1.00	0.32
XIMB	33.10	3.62	34.21	4.44	−1.51	0.14
XLRI	32.21	4.40	33.72	4.44	−3.41	0.00

Note: N = 791; Significance levels of 0.05 and above are considered adequate to indicate significant shift in mean values from entry to exit stage (indicating significant impact of the B-Schools).

Intentionality (INT)

Intentionality refers to the consistency between precept and practise. It also refers to consistency between one's professional goals, values, and decision making. People with high Intentionality are capable of staying focused, despite distractions. They relentlessly pursue their objectives without giving up. Such people are clear about their own motives and use the same to make things happen.

The mean scores at the entry level (see Table 3.3) across the schools on intentionality are noticed to be in the 'very poor' zone[4]. Comparison of the entry and exit stage scores indicates that except IIMA, IIML, and XIMB, in all other cases (MDI, S. P. Jain, Bajaj, IIMB, IIMC, and XLRI) the scores have moved in a positive direction. However, it is important to highlight that significant improvement has occurred only in the case of two schools—MDI and S. P. Jain.

Table 3.3 **Intentionality: means, standard deviation, and T values**

B-Schools	Entry		Exit		t	Sig.
	m	sd	m	sd		
Bajaj	39.05	4.38	40.13	4.43	−2.32	0.02
IIMA	37.61	4.77	36.98	4.44	1.33	0.19
IIMB	38.14	4.92	38.51	5.14	−0.75	0.46
IIMC	38.60	4.64	39.03	3.40	−0.98	0.33
IIML	39.45	4.85	38.90	4.98	1.17	0.25
MDI	37.75	4.78	39.25	4.88	−3.27	0.00
S. P. Jain	39.72	4.29	40.73	4.29	−2.08	0.04
XIMB	39.26	4.36	38.67	4.96	0.83	0.41
XLRI	38.55	4.72	39.06	4.47	−1.17	0.25

Note: N = 791; Significance levels of 0.05 and above are considered adequate to indicate significant shift in mean values from entry to exit stage (indicating significant impact of the B-Schools).

Resilience (RESI)

Resilience refers to psychological toughness to cope with adversity and failures. People with high resilience have the capability to bounce back, retain their curiosity and sense of hope about the future.

Entry levels scores on Resilience (Table 3.4) have been in the 'Good' zone[5] across all the schools barring IIMA and IIMB samples. Further perusal of the table indicates that at the exit level, the scores have improved in all the B-Schools, except in case of IIMC and IIML.

Table 3.4 **Resilience: means, standard deviation, and T values**

B-Schools	Entry		Exit		t	Sig.
	m	sd	m	sd		
Bajaj	37.47	3.86	38.74	3.81	−2.67	0.01
IIMA	36.81	4.56	37.35	4.29	−1.06	0.29
IIMB	36.97	3.88	37.03	4.44	−0.13	0.89
IIMC	37.83	4.10	37.72	3.55	0.26	0.79
IIML	38.36	4.37	37.91	4.60	1.11	0.27
MDI	37.71	4.03	38.31	4.35	−1.57	0.12
S. P. Jain	38.76	3.29	39.26	4.09	−0.98	0.33
XIMB	37.83	3.56	39.10	5.35	−1.86	0.07
XLRI	38.48	4.44	38.57	4.95	−0.17	0.87

Note: N = 791; Significance levels of 0.05 and above are considered adequate to indicate significant shift in mean values from entry to exit stage (indicating significant impact of the B-Schools).

Significant improvement has however been observed in this table only in the case of Bajaj. In other cases, however, the shifts in scores (whether positive or negative) have been insignificant.

Positive outlook (PO)

Positive outlook is viewed as one's ability to see the world in a positive light. People with high score on this dimension demonstrate optimism and confidence; however, people scoring low on this attribute tend to be pessimistic thus leading to feelings of futility and gloom.

Perusal of the entry level scores (Table 3.5) indicates that graduates across the nine schools join with good scores[6]. Some improvement is visible from entry to exit scores in the samples from Bajaj, MDI, and S. P. Jain. However, out of nine schools only in one case (Bajaj) the score has significantly improved. In other samples—IIMA, IIMB, IIMC, and IIML—the scores indicate the negative shift. In fact, there is a significant negative shift in the case of XLRI.

Compassion (COMP)

Compassion refers to the ability to be exceptionally empathetic, to value and appreciate others feelings, and

Table 3.5 **Positive outlook: means, standard deviation, and T values**

B-Schools	Entry		Exit		t	Sig.
	m	sd	m	sd		
Bajaj	28.01	2.77	28.91	2.57	−2.90	0.00
IIMA	27.18	3.70	26.58	3.75	1.70	0.09
IIMB	27.01	4.04	26.78	3.92	0.63	0.53
IIMC	27.98	2.83	27.87	2.92	0.29	0.77
IIML	27.81	3.26	27.21	3.81	1.66	0.10
MDI	27.74	3.43	28.18	3.40	−1.50	0.14
S. P. Jain	28.29	2.94	28.61	3.09	−1.00	0.30
XIMB	27.98	3.33	27.24	3.99	1.31	0.20
XLRI	28.12	3.36	27.15	3.74	2.72	0.01

Note: N = 791; Significance levels of 0.05 and above are considered adequate to indicate significant shift in mean values from entry to exit stage (indicating significant impact of the B-Schools).

view points. In other words, it indicates one's capability to put oneself in the shoes of others and understand their feelings and views from their perspective.

Graduates across the nine schools enter the B-School with 'Poor' scores[7] on this attribute (see Table 3.6). Comparison between entry and exit level scores indicate a positive shift across all the schools. Further analysis of this table, however, indicates that only in one case—Bajaj—the mean score has significantly improved from Round 1 to Round 2.

Table 3.6 Compassion: means, standard deviation, and T values

B-Schools	Entry		Exit		t	Sig.
	m	sd	m	sd		
Bajaj	28.24	3.03	29.36	3.07	−3.40	0.00
IIMA	27.29	2.94	27.67	3.14	−1.10	0.27
IIMB	27.42	3.29	28.07	4.04	1.36	0.18
IIMC	28.02	2.99	28.32	3.14	−0.80	0.45
IIML	28.32	3.65	28.30	3.23	0.07	0.94
MDI	27.76	3.55	28.27	3.32	1.65	0.10
S. P. Jain	28.48	2.97	28.82	3.11	0.96	0.34
XIMB	28.27	2.65	28.50	3.34	0.55	0.59
XLRI	28.44	3.53	28.49	3.19	0.13	0.90

Note: N = 791; Significance levels of 0.05 and above are considered adequate to indicate significant shift in mean values from entry to exit stage (indicating significant impact of the B-Schools).

In sum, the strengths of the graduates lie in their very good scores on emotional awareness of others, good scores on emotional self awareness, positive outlook and resilience (with some exceptions). Graduates thus have excellent ability to observe others emotional state, which is one of the important requirements for managing self in any interaction with individuals and groups.

They also have good capability to understand their own state which in turns aids them in better self regulation. Their positive outlook brings optimism in dealing with difficult situations.

They are, however, weak on intentionality capability, i.e., poor on ability to focus and persevere. This leads to getting distracted or bored when things do not move fast, leading to a tendency to give up and move on to something else rather than persevering and achieving the result. It is worthwhile to mention that relentless perseverance and tenacity are extremely important for providing effective leadership. Their poor compassion score—that is the ability to empathize with others by keeping one's own feelings aside—may make them appear to be self centered and unfeeling thus affecting their capability to reach people when in trouble—this competency is at the very heart of building deeper connections with the team members—the hallmark of leadership.

The overall score on managing self[8] (Table 3.7) reveals a disturbing trend. Only two schools have shown significant improvement on managing self competency, through B-School experience—Bajaj and MDI. In the other schools—IIMB, IIMC, S. P. Jain, though there have been positive shifts, they have been insignificant. In the case of IIMA, IIML, XIMB, and XLRI, in fact, the scores have gone down.

The positive point, however, is that graduates have good scores at the entry level on four of the six attributes and hence this is not too much of a cause for concern. The area of concern, however, are the 'Poor' scores on

Table 3.7 **Managing self—school-wise combined means, standard deviation, and T values**

Schools	Entry		Exit		t	Sig.
	Mean	sd	Mean	sd		
Bajaj	30.98	2.33	31.98	2.45	−4.16	0.00
IIMA	30.08	2.88	29.96	2.82	0.45	0.66
IIMB	30.23	2.87	30.64	3.11	−1.48	0.14
IIMC	30.84	2.31	31.07	2.35	−0.95	0.35
IIML	31.26	2.82	31.03	3.12	0.88	0.38
MDI	30.58	2.86	31.36	2.96	−3.41	0.01
S. P. Jain	31.52	2.30	32.05	2.40	−1.95	0.06
XIMB	31.19	2.18	31.31	3.26	−0.29	0.77
XLRI	30.98	2.84	31.24	2.77	−1.01	0.32

Note: N = 791; Significance levels of 0.05 and above are considered adequate to indicate significant shift in mean values from entry to exit stage (indicating significant impact of the B-Schools).

intentionality and compassion which have been poor at the entry stage and continue to be so at the exit stage.

2. INFLUENCING OTHERS

Capability to influence others is at the core of leadership. It is this capacity which enthuses, galvanizes, and mobilizes people to achieve organizational goals. Leaders influence others through the power of emotional expression, interpersonal connection, constructive discontent, and trust. In this section, the graduates' scores on these four attributes are examined across the nine schools.

Emotional expression (EMEXP)

Emotional expression refers to free expression of emotions, feelings, and gut-level instincts, as and when required. This capability helps leaders to powerfully connect and develop rapport with others and thereby enables them to influence others.

Perusal of Table 3.8 indicates that in the case of seven B-Schools, graduates join with poor scores on

Table 3.8 **Emotional expression: means, standard deviation, and T values**

B-Schools	Entry		Exit		t	Sig.
	m	sd	m	sd		
Bajaj	23.73	3.38	24.51	3.18	−1.99	0.05
IIMA	21.84	3.70	22.77	3.82	−2.59	0.01
IIMB	22.68	3.23	23.53	3.93	−2.19	0.03
IIMC	23.03	3.44	23.73	3.19	−1.65	0.10
IIML	23.48	3.26	22.84	3.84	1.75	0.08
MDI	22.02	3.55	22.87	3.48	−2.55	0.01
S. P. Jain	23.92	3.72	24.51	3.63	−1.53	0.12
XIMB	23.35	2.80	23.28	3.36	0.15	0.88
XLRI	22.89	3.36	23.24	3.34	−1.14	0.26

Note: N = 791; Significance levels of 0.05 and above are considered adequate to indicate significant shift in mean values from entry to exit stage (indicating significant impact of the B-Schools).

this attribute and also leave the schools with scores in the 'poor' zone[9]. However, this is not so in the case of Bajaj and S. P. Jain where the scores are in the 'good' zone at both entry and exit stages.

Examining the impact of B-Schools training, however, indicates that B-School exposure has had a significant positive impact on graduates of four schools—Bajaj, IIMA, IIMB and MDI.

In the case of S. P. Jain, IIMC, and XLRI though the scores have improved, they are not statistically significant. As against this, the scores of IIML and XIMB samples demonstrate negative (though insignificant) shifts. The key concern area is the fact that neither do students come in with good scores, generally speaking, nor does B-School experience help them to develop this competency.

Interpersonal connection (IPC)

Interpersonal connection connotes capability to create and sustain a network of people with whom one has developed authentic relationships. People with high capability display caring, appreciating behaviour as well as sharing hopes, and vulnerabilities. Leadership is nothing but connectedness which binds and bonds people together, thus facilitating smooth movement in the desired direction.

Examination of Table 3.9 brings out low range scores[10] at both, the entry level as well as exit level for all schools barring S. P. Jain where the scores are good at both the entry as well as exit stages. Comparative analysis of means at entry and exit level reveals that graduates of Bajaj, IIMB and IIMC, MDI, and S. P. Jain have improved their scores. However, further analysis of this table indicates that only one school—MDI—has had a significant positive impact on the sample score.

Scores of the graduates of four schools—IIMA, IIML, XIMB, and XLRI—have demonstrated declining shift

Table 3.9 **Interpersonal connections: means, standard deviation, and T values**

B-Schools	Entry		Exit		t	Sig.
	m	sd	m	sd		
Bajaj	23.79	2.58	24.30	2.70	−1.87	0.07
IIMA	22.74	2.79	22.20	3.29	1.69	0.09
IIMB	22.70	3.52	23.10	3.05	−1.34	0.19
IIMC	23.49	2.90	23.60	3.06	−0.30	0.77
IIML	23.46	2.81	23.00	3.35	1.40	0.17
MDI	22.99	3.21	23.70	3.09	−2.49	0.01
S. P. Jain	24.34	2.88	24.20	2.67	0.33	0.74
XIMB	23.76	2.65	22.30	2.73	3.55	0.00
XLRI	23.56	2.94	22.60	3.17	2.97	0.00

Note: $N = 791$; Significance levels of 0.05 and above are considered adequate to indicate significant shift in mean values from entry to exit stage (indicating significant impact of the B-Schools).

from entry to exit stage, the shift being significant in the case of XIMB and XLRI.

Constructive discontent (CONSDIS)

Constructive discontent indicates the capability to stay calm, focused and emotionally grounded even in the face of disagreements and conflicts and convert the conflict in a constructive direction. Conflicts and disagreements are the realities of everyday life. This is so because organizations constitute people with myriad backgrounds, perspectives, attitudes and styles. People who can harmonize, synthesize, and effectively channelize such diverse energies towards coherent goals, stand to emerge as influential leaders.

Similar trend of 'low' zone scores[11] at entry level are evident on constructive discontent (see Table 3.10). This trend continues even at the exit stage. Analysis of this table further reveals that though graduates of all the schools have improved their scores on this attribute at the exit stage, however in the case of Bajaj, IIMB, IIML, MDI, and XIMB, the shift has been significant.

Trust radius (TR)

Trust Radius refers to one's disposition to view others as trustworthy and inherently good. People with high

Table 3.10 **Constructive discontent: means, standard deviation, and T values**

B-Schools	Entry		Exit		t	Sig.
	m	sd	m	sd		
Bajaj	20.80	3.05	22.79	3.43	−5.61	0.00
IIMA	20.76	3.31	21.34	3.25	−1.78	0.80
IIMB	20.77	2.92	22.25	3.85	−3.78	0.00
IIMC	22.06	3.14	22.78	2.76	−1.94	0.06
IIML	21.46	3.40	22.59	3.24	−3.54	0.00
MDI	20.47	3.31	21.97	3.27	−4.67	0.00
S. P. Jain	22.10	3.51	22.67	3.14	−1.43	0.16
XIMB	20.45	3.01	21.70	3.69	−2.50	0.02
XLRI	21.11	3.17	21.36	3.49	−0.74	0.46

Note: N = 791; Significance levels of 0.05 and above are considered adequate to indicate significant shift in mean values from entry to exit stage (indicating significant impact of the B-Schools).

trust radius therefore tend to take people at face value, start on a positive note until there is a reason to do otherwise. The adage goes 'trust begets trust', which is extremely important for influencing people.

Scores on Trust Radius as revealed in Table 3.11 highlight that the students enter as well as exit the B-School with poor scores[12] on this attribute. Analysis of this table brings out that in the case of four school samples—Bajaj, MDI, S. P. Jain, and XIMB—the scores indicate positive shifts. However, only in two cases—Bajaj and MDI—the shifts in scores from entry to exit level have been significant.

Table 3.11   **Trust radius: means, standard deviation, and T values**

B-Schools	Entry		Exit		t	Sig.
	m	sd	m	sd		
Bajaj	29.61	3.68	30.80	3.57	−3.05	0.00
IIMA	29.62	3.95	28.73	4.41	1.97	0.50
IIMB	29.37	3.99	29.23	4.66	0.30	0.77
IIMC	30.61	3.66	30.28	3.40	0.71	0.48
IIML	30.21	3.55	29.23	4.62	2.51	0.01
MDI	30.05	4.01	30.99	3.93	−2.53	0.01
S. P. Jain	30.30	4.00	30.81	4.15	−1.21	0.23
XIMB	29.55	3.69	29.91	3.45	−0.73	0.47
XLRI	30.54	4.18	29.13	4.03	3.26	0.00

Note: N = 791; Significance levels of 0.05 and above are considered adequate to indicate significant shift in mean values from entry to exit stage (indicating significant impact of the B-Schools).

Further perusal indicates that in the case of five—IIMA, IIMB, IIMC, IIML, and XLRI—of the nine schools, the scores have further declined. However, this decline has been significant in the case of two school samples—IIML and XLRI; while in the rest, the decline has been insignificant.

Influencing others—graduates scores on the four attributes of influencing others—emotional expression, interpersonal connection, constructive discontent and trust radius—are in the poor zone at both the entry and exit levels, barring one or two schools.

Table 3.12 indicates that the overall analysis (combined scores) on influencing others (emotional expression, interpersonal connection, constructive discontent and trust) does not present a very happy scenario. Out of the nine schools only two schools—Bajaj and MDI—have shown significant improvement. In the case of IIMB, IIMC and S. P. Jain though the shifts have been positive they are insignificant. Surprisingly, in the case of IIMA, IIML, and XIMB the scores have shifted negatively indicating reduced capability to influence others. The key area of concern is the fact that generally speaking, neither do the students enter schools with good scores

Table 3.12 **Influencing others school-wise combined means, standard deviation, and T values**

B-Schools	Entry		Exit		t	Sig.
	m	sd	m	sd		
Bajaj	24.48	2.33	25.60	2.29	−5.39	0.00
IIMA	23.74	2.59	23.75	2.85	−0.05	0.96
IIMB	23.88	2.75	24.54	3.01	−2.62	0.01
IIMC	24.8	2.47	25.09	2.31	−1.01	0.32
IIML	24.65	2.45	24.42	2.96	0.93	0.35
MDI	23.88	2.63	24.87	2.65	−4.28	0.00
S. P. Jain	25.17	2.68	23.52	2.48	5.88	0.00
XIMB	24.28	2.14	24.29	2.31	−0.03	0.98
XLRI	24.52	2.56	24.08	2.60	1.88	0.06

Note: N = 791; Significance levels of 0.05 and above are considered adequate to indicate significant shift in mean values from entry to exit stage (indicating significant impact of the B-Schools).

(in Influencing Others), nor do the schools heighten this capability.

3. Managing complexity

We are living in the age of discontinuity. Tectonic shifts, unpredictability of the future are a given reality today. The only certainty in today's world is uncertainty, ambiguity, and complexity. Today's world, therefore, needs leaders with the immense capability to navigate through and make sense of such complexities. Those who succeed in doing this find the opportunities amidst the complexities and use them for creating wealth. In this section, we examine creativity and intuition—the two components for managing complexity.

• Creativity (CR)

Creativity refers to the ability to come up with new and different ways to solve problems. People with such ability are non-linear in their approach; they chart new paths, move from red ocean strategy to blue ocean strategy and constantly strive to do things differently. They are constantly in search of new ideas and new solutions to problems and challenges. It is such people who are at ease in complex situations and, therefore, able to see multiple view points and come up with novel solutions.

A study of Table 3.13 indicates that both the entry level as well as exit level scores of the samples are in the 'good' zone[13]. It is heartening to note that B-School training has positively impacted the graduates and enhances their creativity. In all the nine schools, the shifts of scores from entry to exit level have been significant and positive, barring MDI and XIMB.

Table 3.13 Creativity: means, standard deviation, and T values

B-Schools	Entry		Exit		t	Sig.
	m	sd	m	sd		
Bajaj	30.29	3.79	31.65	3.37	–3.14	0.00
IIMA	29.75	3.76	31.16	3.61	–3.54	0.00
IIMB	30.02	3.43	31.26	3.57	–2.60	0.01
IIMC	30.09	3.61	31.53	3.49	–3.35	0.00
IIML	31.01	4.06	32.06	3.91	–2.88	0.01
MDI	30.22	4.05	30.95	4.29	–1.88	0.06
S. P. Jain	31.16	3.40	32.45	3.84	–2.89	0.01
XIMB	30.20	3.54	31.10	4.10	–1.59	0.12
XLRI	30.17	4.14	31.50	3.98	–3.19	0.00

Note: N = 791; Significance levels of 0.05 and above are considered adequate to indicate significant shift in mean values from entry to exit stage (indicating significant impact of the B-Schools).

• Intuition (IN)

Intuition refers to the use of non-cognitive processes—hunches; gut level reactions, and the sixth sense.

People with high ability on this attribute are capable of going beyond logic and analysis. They use their sixth sense, to navigate through potentially overwhelming or conflicting information and derive important insights as well as sense opportunities. This attribute is essential to cope with the uncertainties and complexities and transcend the analysis—paralysis syndrome, which many people experience when they are confronted with complexity.

Analysis of Table 3.14 reveals low scores[14] both, at the entry and the exit levels. Further examination of the table indicates positive shift in eight of the nine B-School samples, the exception being S. P. Jain. In this

Table 3.14   **Intuition: means, standard deviation, and T values**

B-Schools	Entry		Entry		t	Sig.
	m	sd	m	sd		
Bajaj	25.91	3.56	27.73	3.42	−4.75	0.00
IIMA	24.35	4.07	26.05	4.13	−4.00	0.00
IIMB	25.80	3.70	26.78	4.01	−2.13	0.04
IIMC	25.99	3.41	26.12	3.44	−0.28	0.78
IIML	25.99	4.05	26.99	4.29	−2.75	0.01
MDI	25.59	3.92	26.71	4.08	−3.06	0.00
S. P. Jain	26.34	2.87	25.06	3.64	3.38	0.01
XIMB	25.71	3.35	26.20	4.52	−0.83	0.41
XLRI	25.86	3.86	26.95	3.51	−2.71	0.00

Note: N = 791; Significance levels of 0.05 and above are considered adequate to indicate significant shift in mean values from entry to exit stage (indicating significant impact of the B-Schools).

case, scores have significantly reduced at the exit stage. In other six schools—Bajaj, IIMA, IIMB, IIML, MDI, and XLRI—the scores have significantly improved. However, in the case of two schools—IIMC and XIMB—though the scores have improved, the shift has not been statistically significant.

Table 3.15 brings out the school-wise impact on the combined mean score on managing complexity. The significant T values obtained by eight of the nine schools makes it clear that the biggest contribution of the B-Schools lies in developing capability among the graduates to manage complexity.

Table 3.15 **Managing complexity—school-wise combined means, standard deviation, and T values**

B-Schools	Entry		Exit		t	Sig.
	m	sd	m	sd		
Bajaj	28.10	3.01	29.69	2.81	−4.88	0.00
IIMA	27.05	3.56	28.61	3.47	−4.50	0.00
IIMB	27.91	3.11	29.02	3.29	−3.13	0.00
IIMC	28.04	2.98	28.82	2.92	−2.31	0.02
IIML	28.50	3.61	29.52	3.52	−3.34	0.00
MDI	27.91	3.42	28.83	3.72	−2.97	0.00
S. P. Jain	28.75	2.99	30.33	3.34	−4.75	0.00
XIMB	27.96	2.89	28.65	3.66	−1.49	0.14
XLRI	28.01	3.52	29.23	3.56	−3.41	0.00

Note: N = 791; Significance levels of 0.05 and above are considered adequate to indicate significant shift in mean values from entry to exit stage (indicating significant impact of the B-Schools).

4. Managing diversity

For the first time in human history, the world has become truly boundary less. It has brought together people of different cultures, beliefs, ethnic, and religious backgrounds and different values. While this has thrown up opportunities, it has also heightened the potential for disagreement and conflicts. If this diversity is not appropriately harmonized and managed, it can create difficulties in living and working together. Needless to say the power of leadership lies in unifying and integrating diverse forces and using them for creating synergy. Effective integration of divergent forces needs higher tolerance of ambiguity and greater flexibility, which are examined hereafter in the section.

Tolerance–Intolerance of ambiguity (TIA)

The litmus test of leadership is managing the unknown. People with this capability demonstrate competency to grapple with uncertainties, ambiguities, complexities, and discern patterns which may not be normally visible to others. The business world is getting more chaotic (full of competitors) some visible and many invisible. In fact, today's business scenario is too complex to be objectively quantified, and is characterized by subjective realities held by multiple stakeholders—customers, shareholders, employees and society. Leaders with high degree of tolerance for ambiguity do not get anxious or unnerved by such diverse realities and carve out business opportunities out of all the problems characterized by uncertainities and ambiguities. They respond to uncertainty and complexity with unbridled curiosity. In fact, they seem to feel stimulated by ambiguous (unclear) situations and therefore engage with it and explore it. As a result, they are able to discern new patterns in situations characterized by diverse views as well as diverse and dynamic conditions and arrive at new solutions, which enable better problem solving.

Perusal of Table 3.16 brings out that the mean scores are in the average zone[15]. Significant shifts have taken place from entry stage to exit stage in all the schools with the exception of XIMB, where there has been insignificant shift. In the other eight schools, tolerance of ambiguity has significantly improved, the only exception being S. P. Jain. In this case, graduates have become significantly intolerant of ambiguity—in fact, the score has shifted from the average zone at the entry level, to the high zone at the exit level. Thus by and large, B-School exposure has resulted in improved tolerance of ambiguity thus providing greater ability to manage diversity. It would, however, be worthwhile to mention that the scores continue to be in the average zone.

Table 3.16 **Tolerance–Intolerance of ambiguity: means, standard deviation, and T values**

B-Schools	Entry		Exit		t	Sig.
	m	sd	m	sd		
Bajaj	56.30	8.89	51.15	8.65	5.26	0.00
IIMA	52.81	9.36	49.62	8.49	3.31	0.00
IIMB	51.39	8.20	48.55	8.66	2.34	0.02
IIMC	50.98	7.83	47.76	6.50	3.54	0.00
IIML	52.20	9.22	48.85	7.70	4.16	0.00
MDI	55.39	7.08	48.98	9.83	8.24	0.00
S. P. Jain	52.40	9.35	58.21	12.30	−4.00	0.00
XIMB	57.21	9.01	51.52	9.38	4.71	0.00
XLRI	50.64	8.29	50.22	8.93	0.43	0.67

Note: N = 791; Significance levels of 0.05 and above are considered adequate to indicate significant shift in mean values from entry to exit stage (indicating significant impact of the B-Schools). Higher the score greater the intolerance of ambiguity.

Flexibility

Flexibility refers to adaptability to newness, change, and variety. People with higher scores on flexibility are comfortable with newness, change, and variety and are hence better able to deal with diversity in situations and across people, since they are able to listen, explore and make the needed changes in perspectives and actions when required. This enables survival as opposed to Dinosaurian extinction. This is the opposite of rigidity where no matter what the situation demands, the individual is unwilling and perhaps unable, to make the needed shift in viewpoint and approach more in alignment with the new realities. Managing flexibility is therefore the vital component for managing change, innovation, and harmonizing dialectic forces.

Perusal of Table 3.17 brings out that the scores on Flexibility are in the average zone[16] across the nine B-schools. Further analysis brings out that in the case of three schools—IIMB, IIML and XIMB—flexibility has improved as indicated by the reduction in the scores. In fact, the IIML graduates have significantly improved their flexibility. In the other seven schools, however,

Table 3.17 **Flexibility: means, standard deviation, and T values**

B-Schools	Entry		Exit		t	Sig.
	m	sd	m	sd		
Bajaj	45.78	6.30	45.82	6.36	−0.10	0.94
IIMA	43.53	7.04	43.81	7.64	−0.40	0.68
IIMB	43.12	5.88	42.98	6.95	0.20	0.85
IIMC	42.11	5.76	43.39	6.26	−2.00	0.05
IIML	45.63	5.86	44.13	6.70	2.74	0.01
MDI	44.29	6.34	43.73	6.51	0.96	0.34
S. P. Jain	42.86	6.90	44.49	7.02	−2.00	0.05
XIMB	45.29	7.26	45.13	6.97	0.18	0.86
XLRI	42.82	6.32	43.84	7.31	−1.60	0.12

Note: N = 791; Significance levels of 0.05 and above are considered adequate to indicate significant shift in mean values from entry to exit stage (indicating significant impact of the B-Schools); Lower the score greater the flexibility.

though the scores have moved towards greater inflexibility, they are not statistically significant. Only in two cases—IIMC and S. P. Jain—the scores have been statistically significant. Thus, by and large, B-School experience has contributed to making graduates less flexible as compared to the entry levels, thus affecting their capability to manage diversity.

Inculcating competence to handle complexity appears to be the greatest strength of the Super-League B-Schools. Analysis of the combined score on managing complexity (creativity and intuition) presented in Table 3.18 brings out that of the nine schools, graduates

Table 3.18 **Managing diversity—school-wise means, standard deviations, and T values**

B-Schools	Entry		Exit		t	Sig.
	m	sd	m	sd		
Bajaj	36.96	4.71	35.70	4.72	2.99	0.00
IIMA	34.97	5.25	34.31	5.33	1.35	0.18
IIMB	34.41	4.23	33.63	4.81	1.43	0.16
IIMC	33.80	4.14	33.63	4.08	0.37	0.72
IIML	35.86	4.48	34.28	4.53	4.22	0.00
MDI	34.40	4.373	28.52	3.46	18.71	0.00
S. P. Jain	34.53	5.00	36.79	5.37	−3.79	0.00
XIMB	36.95	5.52	35.44	5.12	2.42	0.02
XLRI	34.07	4.64	34.48	5.26	−0.83	0.41

Note: N = 791; Significance levels of 0.05 and above are considered adequate to indicate significant shift in mean values from entry to exit stage (indicating significant impact of the B-Schools).

of eight have significantly improved their scores from the entry to exit levels, the sole exception being XIMB. Even in this case the score has improved although it is insignificant.

5. Impact of B-School experience on the four leadership dimensions: Overall view across the nine schools

Table 3.19 presents the comparative picture of the impact of the nine B-Schools on the four competency dimensions—managing self, influencing others, managing complexity, and managing diversity. Analysis of this table indicates that there are only two schools—Bajaj and MDI—which have significantly impacted the scores across all the four dimensions. These two schools are followed by IIML where, the impact has been on two of the four dimensions—Managing Complexity and Managing Diversity. As against these, schools like IIMA, IIMB, IIMC, S. P. Jain, and XLRI—have significantly impacted on only one dimension—Managing Complexity. The impact of XIMB has been only on one dimension—Managing Diversity.

These findings bring out that most of India's lead schools (7 out of 9 approximately; 78 per cent) have not succeeded in significantly shaping the mindsets of the

Table 3.19 Means, standard deviation, and T values of the four dimensions: managing self, influencing others, managing complexity, and managing diversity

	Managing self						Influencing others					
	rd1 mean	SD	rd2 mean	SD	t	Sig.	rd1 mean	SD	rd2 mean	SD	t	Sig.
Bajaj	30.98	2.33	31.98	2.45	-4.16	0.00	24.48	2.33	25.60	2.27	-5.39	0.00
IIMA	30.08	2.88	29.96	2.82	0.45	0.66	23.74	2.59	23.75	2.85	-0.05	0.96
IIMB	30.23	2.87	30.64	3.11	-1.48	0.14	23.88	2.75	24.54	3.01	-2.62	0.01
IIMC	30.84	2.31	31.07	2.35	-0.95	0.35	24.80	2.47	25.09	2.31	-1.01	0.32
IIML	31.26	2.82	31.03	3.12	0.88	0.38	24.65	2.45	24.42	2.96	0.93	0.35
MDI	30.58	2.86	31.36	2.96	-3.41	0.00	23.88	2.63	24.87	2.65	-4.28	0.00
S. P. Jain	31.52	2.30	32.05	2.40	-1.95	0.06	25.17	2.68	23.52	2.48	5.88	0.00
XIMB	31.19	2.18	31.31	3.26	-0.29	0.77	24.28	2.14	24.29	2.31	-0.03	0.98
XLRI	30.98	2.84	31.24	2.77	-1.01	0.32	24.52	2.56	24.08	2.60	1.88	0.06
Bajaj	28.10	3.01	29.69	2.81	-4.88	0.00	36.96	4.71	35.70	4.72	2.99	0.00
IIMA	27.05	3.56	28.61	3.47	-4.5	0.00	34.97	5.25	34.31	5.33	1.35	0.18
IIMB	27.91	3.11	29.02	3.29	-3.13	0.00	34.41	4.23	33.63	4.81	1.42	0.16
IIMC	28.04	2.98	28.82	2.92	-2.31	0.02	33.80	4.14	33.63	4.08	0.37	0.72

(Continued)

(Continued)

	Managing self						Influencing others					
	rd1 mean	SD	rd2 mean	SD	t	Sig.	rd1 mean	SD	rd2 mean	SD	t	Sig.
IIML	28.50	3.61	29.52	3.52	−3.34	0.00	35.86	4.48	34.28	4.53	4.22	0.00
MDI	27.91	3.42	28.83	3.72	−2.97	0.00	34.40	4.373	28.52	3.46	18.71	0.00
S. P. Jain	28.75	2.99	30.33	3.34	−4.75	0.00	34.53	5.00	36.79	5.37	−3.79	0.00
XIMB	27.96	2.89	28.65	3.66	−1.49	0.14	36.95	5.52	35.44	5.12	2.42	0.02
XLRI	28.01	3.52	29.23	3.56	−3.41	0.00	34.07	4.64	34.48	5.26	−0.83	0.41

Note: N = 791.

B-School graduates on the selected dimensions critical for leadership—managing self, influencing others, managing complexity, and managing diversity.

SUMMARY AND CONCLUSIONS

The following salient conclusions emerge from the findings of the chapter:

1. **Managing Self:**

   (a) B-School graduates enter the school with very good scores on emotional awareness of others, good scores on emotional self awareness, resilience and positive outlook. They also by and large leave the school with the scores in the same range, i.e. good, as at the entry level.

   (b) Scores of B-School graduates are found to be very poor on intentionality and poor on compassion at both entry and exit stages.

2. **Influencing Others**

   (a) Scores on influencing others are found to be poor on all the four sub-dimensions— emotional expression, interpersonal connections, constructive discontent and trust radius. Scores on these sub-dimensions continue to be in the poor zone in most of the cases at the exit stage irrespective of statistically significant shifts.

3. **Managing Complexity**

   (a) On the attribute of creativity, graduates in B-Schools enter with good scores which are further significantly influenced through B-Schools' exposure in most of the cases. The scores at the exit stage continue to be in the same zone (good) as the entry stage.

   (b) Graduates enter the B-Schools with poor scores on intuition. However, B-Schools' exposure in this case helps in significantly improving their scores, although the score does not shift into the good zone.

4. **Managing Diversity**

   (a) On both the sub-dimensions, flexibility and tolerance of ambiguity—students enter the B-Schools with average scores.

   (b) In the case of tolerance of ambiguity, most schools have significant impact in improving the scores.

   (c) In the case of flexibility, graduates' scores have not been significantly impacted and the scores continue to be similar to those at the entry level.

Out of nine schools, only two schools have significantly impacted the managerial competencies across all the four dimensions—managing self, influencing others, managing complexity, and managing diversity. As against this, most of the schools have impacted on only one dimension—managing complexity. This indicates a major failure of B-Schools in shaping graduates for managing self, influencing others, and managing diversity.

Similar findings have also emerged at the perceived level from both the corporate executives as well as the alumni samples (see Chapter 2). In fact, this data further reinforces the findings of the psychometric tests discussed in this chapter. Such findings conclusively bring out the major concerns about the quality of exposure provided by B-Schools in shaping the mindset of the graduates to be future leaders.

These findings broadly support the concerns raised by corporate leaders, B-School alumni, accreditation institutions, and management thinkers. The findings conclusively bring out the need for radical reform in management education to develop future leaders.

NOTES

1. Data was collected at Entry level as well as at Exit level from each of the nine B-Schools under study. For details of measures and definitions, please see Chapter 1, Appendix 1.

2. ESA Scores range: 19.14 to 22.88 are considered to be in the 'Good' zone.

3. EAO Score range: 30.72 and above are in the 'Very Good' zone.

4. INT Score range: 35.50 and below are considered to be in the 'Very Poor' zone.

5. RESI Score range: 37.30 to 41.57 are in the 'Good' zone.

6. PO Score range: 24.51 to 28.50 are considered to be the 'Good' zone.

7. COMP Score range: 25.14 to 28.88 are considered to be in the 'Poor' zone.

8. Arrived at by cumulating the scores on the six attributes—Emotional Self Awareness, Emotional Awareness of Others, Intentionality, Resilience, Positive Outlook and Compassion.

9. EMEXP Score range: 20 to 23.56 are considered to be in 'Poor' zone.

10. IPC Score range: 19.95 to 24.15 are in the 'Poor' zone.

11. CONSDIS Score range: 20.41 to 24.40 are considered to be in the 'Poor' zone.

12. TR Score range: 26.26 to 31.25 are considered to be the 'Poor' zone.

13. CR Score range: 29.51 to 34.50 are considered to be the 'Good' zone.

14. IN Score range: 23.32 to 27.41 are considered to be the 'Poor' zone.
15. TIA Score ranges: 43 to 56 are considered to be in the average zone.
16. FLEX Score ranges: 38 to 47 in the average zone.

Chapter 4

Conclusions, implications, and new directions

Today, India enjoys unprecedented attention and limelight on the world stage for its talent, its booming economy, and large markets. The latest *Goldman Sachs report* predicts that India will be the second largest economy after China in 2050. The sustained growth of the Indian economy at eight per cent over the last few years has built tremendous confidence in the business community. There is a wave of optimism regarding India's capability to be a leading economic power in the 21st century.

Increasingly, the world is demonstrating intense interest in the Indian economy and choosing India as a preferred investment destination. Even leading global business schools—Harvard, Wharton, London Business School, INSEAD, Kellogg and Darden (among others)—are keen to document the outstanding success stories of the likes of Ratan Tata, Narayana Murthy, Azim Premji, Sunil Mittal, K M Birla, the Ambani brothers, Kiran Mazumdar Shaw, Anji Reddy, and a host of others.

It has been decisively proved that the power of a nation is thus linked to economic power, rather than natural resources or military power. This has been amply demonstrated in the case of Singapore, Japan, and Germany among others. World history also teaches that the power of a nation is linked with the power of mind and leadership ability.

The actualization of the Goldman Sachs prediction will however, depend heavily on India's capability to develop talent and groom leaders of the calibre of Ratan Tata, L N Mittal, Sunil Mittal, K M Birla, Mukesh Ambani, Anil Ambani, etc. Coincidentally, the demographic dividend is in India's favour, the major challenge being to convert the large pool of human resources into future leaders.

Unfortunately, the economic world at large and the corporate world in particular are quite disenchanted with the talent being churned out by schools of higher learning, be it in technology or management. Business leaders, alumni, accrediting institutions and even some management thinkers are almost unanimous in their opinion about the failure of Indian management schools to groom and shape future business leaders of the needed calibre. The above factors were the triggering point for undertaking this work.

In this study, nine lead schools (see Appendices 1a and 1b for the profiles of each school) of the country were chosen. The underlying assumption was that these schools would probably focus on heightening the leadership competencies of the graduates through the superior quality of their programmes. It was also felt that what did not happen in these schools, would certainly not take place in the other schools.

This has been a longitudinal work comprising data collection at two points in time—entry level as well as exit level—on the same population of graduates. In Round 1, data was gathered from 1250 students of Bajaj, IIMA, IIMB, IIMC, IIML, MDI, S P Jain, XLRI, and XIMB. In Round 2, the sample dropped to 800 and ultimately the number of usable responses was 791. This part of the work spanned two years.

The second part of the study—data gathering from stakeholders (alumni of the selected schools as well as corporate executives)—was carried out with a view to understanding the level of responsiveness of management schools to stakeholders' requirements, that is, understanding the perceptions of the stakeholders about the B-School product.

One hundred and ten senior corporate leaders and 334 alumni participated in this study. Data were gathered by using structured questionnaires, in-depth interviews and anthropological inquiry, besides studying the best practices of some leading American B-Schools— Michigan Ann Arbor (Ross School of Business),

Case Western (Weatherhead School of Management), Kellogg, Wharton, and Darden School (UVA). This part of the work took another two years, the total time spanning four years. Thus, data was gathered from multiple stakeholders—students, alumni, corporate leaders, and B-Schools deans and professors.

While there are many competencies vital to provide effective leadership, however in this study, only four have been dealt with:

1. Managing Self,
2. Influencing others,
3. Managing Complexity, and
4. Managing Diversity.

These four leadership dimensions were chosen based on the literature survey and the author's own observations and experiences as a consultant and trainer. In fact, these are the four dimensions which can make or break a leader. Of these, the first dimension is linked with Self—the perspective being that those who cannot manage self cannot manage others. Another vital leadership dimension chosen for this study is Influencing Others—which is at the heart of the business of leading. After all, the role of a leader is to above all, mobilize and galvanize others and channel their energy in the needed direction.

The changing nature of the business terrain and the competitors is such that the business world is getting increasingly murky and unpredictable. This has, therefore, made the business context extremely complex. Hence, providing leadership in such a context means managing complexity, the third dimension assessed in the study. The fourth dimension of this work—Managing Diversity—has today assumed a vital role since the world has become boundary-less, throwing up challenges of enormous diversity in terms of culture, race, ideas, attitudes, and values, not to mention gender and language.

KEY CONCLUSIONS

The following salient conclusions emerge from this research work:

(A) Recruiters views

1. *Perceived strengths of B-School graduates*: B-School graduates have been perceived by the recruiters to have

   (a) high analytical power,
   (b) high self confidence,

(c) excellent communication and presentation skills, along with,

(d) high ability to withstand work pressure, and

(e) capability at quick thinking.

2. Desired vs. perceived strengths of top B-School graduates: Recruiters' views, however, also indicated significant gaps between desired competencies from the B-School graduates and the actual competencies which graduates come with when they join companies. Corporate sector needs graduates who are:

(a) excellent team workers, with

(b) high performance focus. They look for graduates who demonstrate,

(c) high capability to lead along with

(d) analytical power, and

(e) self confidence.

In contrast, recruiters perceive that, B-School graduates are:

(a) poor team workers, low on both,

(b) performance focus, and

(c) capability to lead and mobilize people.

This indicates a strong mismatch between expectations of the corporate world and the perceived reality on the top three competencies demonstrated by the graduates.

3. Perceived attitudes of top B-School graduates: Recruiters have felt that graduates from top schools lack reality orientation regarding the corporate world. They have been found to have:

    (a) individualistic style of functioning, they are
    (b) highly ambitious,
    (c) carry a chip on the shoulder and they have
    (d) poor implementation skills.

4. Competencies required—Future perspective: Business leaders opined that in the near future, corporate world will need leaders with:

    (a) Change management,
    (b) Entrepreneurial abilities,
    (c) Global mindsets, and
    (d) High ambiguity tolerance.

(B) Alumni views

1. Perceived competency development in the B-School: Alumni have expressed the view that

their respective B-Schools have done a fairly good job of inculcating:

(a) Communication and presentation skills,
(b) Analytical ability,
(c) Ability to sustain work pressure,
(d) Problem solving, and
(e) Performance focus.

2. Needed current competencies: Alumni have further suggested that B-Schools should also focus on a set of competencies more in line with today's workplace requirements inculcating:

(a) Global mindset, increasing
(b) Performance focus, developing
(c) Negotiation skills, and equipping graduates at
(d) Quick thinking, and
(e) Working amidst uncertainty.

Alumni are of the opinion that these competencies are critical requirements in the present context and that B-Schools do not pay adequate attention to develop these.

3. Beliefs of the alumni and impact of B-School: B-School exposure significantly heightened the scores on:

(a) Achievement orientation,
(b) People orientation,
(c) Work focus,
(d) Quality orientation,
(e) Ideas and concept focus,
(f) Time orientation, and
(g) Contribution focus.

However, in the case of position and power focus and money and material things, although the scores have increased through B-School exposure, the score shift has not been significant. In the case of integrity, honesty, religious orientation, and aesthetic orientation, unfortunately, the scores have eroded through B-School exposure. It is worthwhile to mention that only in three cases (time orientation, people, and achievement orientation) the scores have moved above the midpoint, post B-School exposure.

4. Work-place challenges for managing career growth and performance and B-School focus:

(a) Delivering timely results,
(b) Managing superior,
(c) Leading team, and
(d) Motivating people,

were the top four challenges identified by the alumni to manage career growth as well as performance. According to the alumni, B-School experience did help to improve their competency on delivering timely results. However, in the case of attributes like, managing superior, leading team, and motivating people, alumni did not experience enough contribution by the B-School. In other words, B-Schools have not equipped graduates with insights and competencies to manage and lead people, which are perceived to be critical both for managing career growth as well as performance.

(C) B-School graduates: profiles (entry and exit levels: self assessment-psychometric) and B-School impact

1. B-School graduates join the programme with reasonably good competency to manage complexity and they have significantly improved on this dimension through the B-School experience.
2. In the case of managing diversity, they enter the B-School with average capability. B-School exposure significantly heightens their capability on this dimension although the scores continue to be in the average zone at the exit level also.

3. On self management competency (comprising emotional awareness of others, emotional self awareness, resilience, positive outlook. Intentionality, and compassion), the overall score of the graduates is average. The graduates' competency is very good at the entry level on emotional awareness of others and they have good scores on emotional self awareness, resilience, and positive outlook. They also, by and large, leave the school with the scores in the same range i.e., good, as at the entry level. Scores of B-School graduates are found to be very poor on intentionality and poor on compassion at both, entry and exit stages. Unfortunately, the graduates join and also leave the B-School with scores in the very poor (intentionality) and poor zone (compassion) on these two attributes of self management.

4. Influencing Others: It is a matter of concern that B-School graduates join with poor scores on influencing others (emotional expression, interpersonal connections, constructive discontent, and trust radius) and worse, they exit with poor scores on these attributes. Considering that influencing others is the primary business of a leader, this finding raises questions about the role and relevance of B-School exposure in grooming leaders.

5. A bird's eye view of the findings across the four leadership dimensions (managing self, influencing others, managing complexity, and managing diversity) across the nine schools again bring out a disappointing picture. Out of nine schools only two schools—Bajaj and MDI—have significantly impacted the managerial competencies across all the four dimensions. Other schools have impacted only one or two dimensions.

6. Findings in this part of the work coincide with the views expressed both by alumni and corporate executives (cited in Part A and B). Such findings conclusively reinforce the major concerns expressed by the various stakeholders regarding the quality of exposure provided by B-Schools' in shaping the mindsets of the graduates to be future leaders.

Viewing the findings in a holistic sense, one is bound to get perturbed and also curious as to what has gone wrong with management education in top B-Schools and what remedial actions could be initiated to heighten the relevance of B-Schools in grooming future leaders.

The above findings conclusively bring out the need for radical reforms in:

(a) Thrust and focus of management education,
(b) Substance and content of management education, and
(c) Pedagogy for delivery.

In the subsequent paragraphs, an attempt is made to map out the road ahead for B-Schools to develop future business leaders. Indian B-Schools need to make the following paradigm shifts to enable development of new mental architecture[1] among the graduates:

FROM	TO
Preponderant Concept Focus	Issue Focus
Preponderant Ideas Focus	Action Focus
Preponderant Cognitive Focus	Emotive Focus
Preponderant Analytical Focus	Holistic World View
Case and Lecture Method	Experiential Learning
Local Mindset	Global Mindset
Career Seeker	Entrepreneurs and Wealth Creator

Concept to issue focus

The prevailing criticism which B-Schools face is regarding the preponderance of concepts, analysis and ideas over issues and problems. Consequently, the core business of management—problem solving and handling issues—get inadequate attention. One has invariably heard the sarcastic comment regarding solutions given by management graduates in the corporate sector—'Oh it's a theoretical solution'. In fact, many recruiters like to tell graduates who join their organizations, 'Our first challenge is to get you to unlearn what you have learnt in the B-School'.

Closer scrutiny of the MBA curriculum and even training programmes (for corporate executives) floated by B-Schools tends to reinforce the conceptual orientation. Many expensive consulting reports gathering dust on corporate shelves are further testimony to the concept centric rather than issue-centric focus. The idea is not to denounce the power of concepts but to highlight the need to integrate concepts with issues and problems faced by the corporate world. It would therefore be desirable for B-Schools (in collaboration with industry) to identify contemporary issues and problems confronted by companies and then do backward integration to work out the relevant inputs and chalk out the course design.

Idea to action focus

Swami Vivekananda's famous quote 'Thought without action doesn't have any value; however action without thought is a futile exercise', powerfully highlights the importance of integrating both, thought and action in management education. It is worthwhile to highlight that in an era of tectonic shifts in the business scenario, the very relevance of theories postulated in the past to handle the present and future issues is under question. The genesis of theory development in the management domain lies in capturing past practices and converting them into concepts and theoretical frameworks. While they are useful snapshots of the past, to use them as frameworks to view the present and future may not be desirable for problem solving. Unfortunately, professors feel very comfortable with models and frameworks evolved on the basis of past realities. The key challenge is to inculcate the mindsets to interact with business realities and then develop appropriate frameworks. Human beings invariably suffer from the syndrome of trained incapacity and, therefore, tend to convert every situation into the existing models and mental frameworks. Therefore, greater exposure to, and transaction with the business world become important for both, students and professors.

To move from preponderant idea centric focus to action centric approach, 50 per cent of each course should be taught by practicing managers. Spending at least a month in a year in the industry using the anthropological mode would deepen the understanding of professors regarding live situations and current challenges in organizations. Therefore, research by B-School professors will have to move from the dominant mode of gathering data for validation of theories typically evolved in the Western context and become an integral part of the current business context. Powerful learning and insights as well as acceptance (from the community) comes when one becomes part of the community that one is serving, rather than by becoming a spectator from the outside.

Cognitive to emotive

Simply put, handling business situations comprises both, quality and acceptance components. While the quality component is linked with the human cognitive map (power of the bright idea), the implementation and acceptance component is linked with their emotive map (people power). Leaders who overemphasize the cognitive power and ignore the emotive power, may fail to galvanize, enthuse, and channel human energy towards implementation of the brilliant ideas. In fact, leadership is nothing but connection and influence, both being rooted in emotive power. Activating, understanding and regulating one's own emotive power can not only enable one to influence others but also to manage oneself.

The reality of management schools, however, is an overemphasis on development of the cognitive map—logic, analysis—to the detriment of development of the emotive map. Such training makes the graduates knowledgeable but with poor capability to lead, since leading primarily emanates from emotive power.

Students need to be provided opportunities to understand their emotive and inner psychic space. When emotive power is not developed, it remains the Dark Continent of the human psyche leading to lack of regulation and utilization of the creative energies. Pedagogies[2] like theatre, outbound, literature experiential labs, and to some extent gaming, will help them tremendously. In fact, these pedagogies further enable overall personality development—understanding self, identifying strengths and weaknesses, building perspectives on life. Since each of the above cited pedagogies involve the complete human being, they force one to confront one's own values and reflect on one's own behaviour. The highly popular pedagogy of a B-School—the case method—needless to say (while having its own merits), is inadequate for developing emotive competencies.

Tunneled perspective to holistic mindset

There is unanimity among world philosophers, statesmen, and management thinkers regarding the qualities which make a good leader. The dominant view appears to be that a leader should have a vision and Himalayan dream. The person should be well versed in literature and philosophy; along with aesthetic sense, artistic temperament and a well-developed value system. Above all, the leader should have a holistic world view encompassing perspective of life, society and the globe.

Examining management education from this perspective indicates that there are many gaps. The preponderant focus is narrow—inculcating a set of analytical tools, techniques and to some extent, business perspective. This increases the narrow specialization and tunneled vision. Graduates of B-Schools therefore do not develop the holistic world perspective that can emerge from understanding historical, social, cultural, political, and environmental factors impacting societies which form the real world context in which they make decisions. In the absence of such exposure, their decision making is myopic. Concern for profit maximization overshadows the concern for the larger context in which the company operates. The contemporary issue of corporate governance—impact of businesses on communities, environment—is a direct reflection of the short sightedness and insensitivity of business leaders towards larger societal issues. To overcome these limitations of Business Education, B-Schools should introduce larger component of liberal arts and social science education in the curriculum to develop broader awareness and appreciation. It would be worthwhile to mention that after years of debate, Harvard faculty have (in 2007) accepted the relevance of culture, religion, and philosophy and have decided to introduce these subjects in the B-School curriculum.

Management schools should identify classical works by social thinkers and philosophers; they should identify autobiographies and biographies of great people; select all-time great films, and use the interaction with great minds as the vehicle to broaden their perspective. This becomes more important in view of the fact that most management graduates preponderantly come from technical, commerce as well as economic streams of education, where they do not get the chance to engage with the arts, philosophy, history, literature, culture, political science, etc.

Most importantly, in the whole process of the above cited educational paradigm, a better human being is developed. Needless to say, world history is ample testimony to the fact that it is evolved persons like Gandhi, Mandela, Martin Luther King, Lincoln, Jefferson, De Gaulle, and others who made the world a better place for subsequent generations. In the business world too, there are fine examples of leaders—Akio Morita, Matsushita, GD Birla, JRD Tata, Bill Gates, Lee Berners, who contributed to make the world a better place. Study of their biographies brings out that they were evolved persons with larger vision, holistic perspective and a sense of community and responsibility towards society.

Lecture to experiential learning

The Confucian dictum, 'when I read I forget, when I see I remember but when I do I understand', brings out the power of experiential learning for behavioural change. Top B-Schools by and large unfortunately tend to overly emphasize case method as a teaching pedagogy. No doubt the case method is a potent vehicle for heightening analytical capability and improving problem-solving skills; it however provides little opportunity to learn by doing. As such it is an inappropriate pedagogy to build behavioural change. Management schools must, therefore, move towards experiential learning, more project-based pedagogies and weekly secondment (at least once a week) with the industry.

Local to global

Crumbling of geopolitical boundaries has rendered the world without boundaries in many ways. For the first time in human history, there is emergence of the global citizen. In such a world, people with global mindset will be able to compete, thrive, and excel. Grooming global citizens is a challenging issue in India unlike Europe and USA where, top schools have diverse student groups. There is no global community of students in most Indian B-Schools. Schools do not make efforts to have a global pool of students. Therefore diversity management capabilities of our students remain underdeveloped. In the present context, it is imperative that B-Schools develop more strategic alliances, exchange programmes of students and faculty, actively attract international students in many top schools of the world.

This will enable them to build a global learning context within the B-School. To do this, however, B-Schools must reframe their own role and self identity and view themselves as global institutions, developing future leaders for the world. They should avoid getting lulled into a false sense of complacency given the heavy local demand for seats in management schools. In fact, it is high time that Indian B-Schools go aggressively for global accreditations—AMBA, EQUIS and AACSB. Ironically, more than 95 per cent of Indian B-Schools do not have national accreditation, let alone global. There is only one school—MDI—which has global accreditation—the AMBA. By opting for global accreditation, B-Schools get the opportunity to learn global processes, systems, strategies, standards, which they can use for benchmarking and continuous improvement.

Career seekers to wealth creators

India is a highly populous country and in the coming years, the growing percentage of youthful population will exert enormous pressure on the economy and society demanding gainful occupation. If this issue is not seriously addressed, there can be social unrest and violence creating enormous fissures in society.

India today needs wealth and job creators rather than job seekers. Regrettably, B-Schools take great pride in publicizing the fat pay packages and quick placements as a badge of achievement. Perhaps, B-Schools see their role more in terms of grooming job seekers rather than job creators. Things have eroded to such an extent that many students and even many recruiters view B-Schools more as employment exchanges—a sad commentary on the relevance of B-Education. It is time that B-Schools aggressively inculcate the entrepreneurial and business mindset among the students. This can be done through various means—floating programmes in the area of entrepreneurship and starting new businesses. The delivery model should consist of scope for idea incubation, mentoring by entrepreneurs, financial institutions, venture capitalists and angel investors. This will provide students practice in identifying business opportunities and framing the context, creating new businesses, and go through the entire gamut from ideation to creation of a new business.

Great institutions are built and sustained based on the power of clarity of the business they are in and effectively aligning their strategies, structure, systems, actions and culture. It is time that B-Schools also define the business they are in. In fact B-Schools are in the business of grooming future leaders and not in the business of teaching finance, marketing, operations or organizational behaviour. It is therefore recommended that a course on leadership be made compulsory for all students. Faculty teaching various courses should also incorporate this approach in all their courses as far as possible. In fact, Wharton has already made Leadership courses mandatory for all students and it is taught in an experiential mode.

Only excellent learning institutions can become excellent teaching institutions. Therefore, it is sine qua non for B-Schools to be learning institutions through continuous feedback from the corporate world, with new ideas, venturing into new fields and continuously asking questions regarding the relevance of what they do vis-à-vis the institutions they are supposed to serve. This can be possible only when there is periodic reflection of what they are doing and also initiating continuous quest for excellence.

Such reflection can be meaningful and its value can be accentuated when this is done in conjunction with their customers and the institutions they are supposed to cater to—all the stakeholders. It is therefore recommended that B-School faculty should periodically get away from the routine and collectively mull over issues their stakeholders are confronted with.

World over, questions are raised about the appropriateness of the GMAT for capturing the attributes relevant for leadership development. Similar questions are raised by management thinkers and practitioners in India about the CAT test, which is heavily quant-centric. The CAT test does not have a robust component to capture the practical, emotional, spiritual, value based, and ethical aspects which are the cornerstones for leadership. In fact, the CAT test is often considered to be a test of elimination rather than a test for selection. To overcome the deficiencies of the CAT, B-Schools will have to develop alternate methods of assessment. This can be possible through simulations, introducing appropriate test batteries, allotting longer time for group discussion, interviews, etc.

Role of corporate sector and alumni

Corporate world and industry have been very critical about the quality of technical education in this country. The perennial criticism about higher education has been that it is unrealistic, out of touch with business requirements, and theoretical. This is a common lament cutting across various segments of society—bureaucracy, political parties, corporate world, alumni, other citizens, etc.

Serious examination of the role (corporate sector and alumni) they have played in supporting high quality education reveals a disappointing scenario. Examining the contribution of corporate sector and alumni in building high quality institutions in the western world brings out a scenario of contrasts. There is a flow of generous grants, besides support through other means to educational institutions. Glaring examples are the endowments given to schools like Kellogg, Wharton, Kelly, Johnson, Ross, Smith, Darden, etc. Schools are also supported through access to the companies for research, case writing, secondments, industry assignments, consulting, etc. In the western world, educational institutions are held in high esteem and even Presidents of countries feel greatly honoured to be invited to address faculty and students of B-Schools.

However, the Indian story is very different—very few individuals and industries come forward to support educational institutions in different ways. It would be worthwhile to mention here that it is ultimately the corporate world which will either benefit from high quality education or pay a heavy price for poor quality. The scenario in the corporate world today is that they hire graduates and then spend considerable time (from six months to one year and more) in training and retraining them—what a colossal waste of time and money. Active involvement and engagement of the corporate world will not only bring down the training costs but also enable them to get students with the best fit for their companies. The story is not very different in the case of alumni (again unlike the West). Unfortunately, there is no concept of giving back (to one's own institutions) which ironically, the Indian tradition views as one's Dharma.

Future move: lessons from global lead schools

Benchmarking and learning from best practices is an important developmental vehicle for change and transformation, for building competitive edge. The usage of this strategy is widespread among growing and changing institutions. An effort has been made here to highlight some of the salient strategies used for development of future business leaders in some of the top schools in USA (visited and studied by the author as part of the postdoctoral Senior Fulbright Research)—Kellogg School (Northwestern), Ross School (Michigan Ann Arbor), Weatherhead School (Case Western), Darden School (UVA), and Wharton School (U Penn):

(a) The aforementioned schools lay emphasis in some way or the other, on individual development. A series of initiatives are undertaken on individual-centric behaviour change and personality development, going far beyond communication and presentation skills. There is heavy accent on development of interpersonal skills, team skills, and leadership in these schools. At Wharton School, the basic organizational behaviour course has been replaced by a course on leadership and team working, which is delivered through use of multiple pedagogical vehicles including simulations and theatre. Sessions involving simulations are typically taught in a class of 30 students. Weather head School, which has been very innovative in the area of leadership development, conducts assessment of capabilities at the entry level, mapping of ideal and actual self, followed by gap analysis and development of an individual leadership development plan. This is periodically monitored and evaluated.

(b) The schools have moved from the typical concept centric to outcome competency centric approach to business education.

(c) Business and entrepreneurship are increasingly becoming the thrust of these schools.

(d) These schools provide 'immersion experiences' where students go in groups to different parts of the world, meet local leaders, and do projects which help provide multicultural and multifunctional experiences leading to holistic thinking and appreciation of diversity.

(e) These schools, notably Ross and Darden, also carry out formal workshops at the end of the programme to prepare students to transit smoothly from the academic world, to the action world. They involve alumni and corporate executives to help in this process by sharing stories of success and failure. Such formal workshops are found useful to develop pragmatic orientation to effectively manage transitions.

(f) These schools are experimenting schools in terms of pedagogy and floating new courses needed by the market. Professors are quite entrepreneurial and are closely involved with the corporate world, working with senior levels of management and this enables them to assess the market trends and respond to them.

(g) These top schools are utilizing the power of theatre, especially interactive theatre. The experiences of acting, directing, working together, and performing before an audience, enable students to become more exploring, utilizing non-linear capabilities, thinking on their feet, understanding their own value systems and assumptions and above all, developing capabilities to work together. In addition, it also helps students to learn to make their presence felt, communicate with impact as well as develop greater self confidence.

(h) Films are used extensively as a vehicle for inculcating values and leadership competencies. Notably at Darden, there are regular fortnightly film shows where different professors make the time to facilitate group discussion, dialogue, and extraction of learning points post the film show. Among other things, this enables students to benchmark themselves against role models.

(i) Some schools, notably Darden also use literature as a vehicle to teach subjects like leadership and ethics.

(j) Special efforts are made to develop cross-functional integration through projects, multidisciplinary courses and team teaching, enabling students to develop holistic business perspective and move away from silo and tunneled vision.

(k) Creation of discussion groups around contemporary issues is a student-led activity which helps to develop holistic thinking, being in touch with the contemporary issues, enable building of environmental sensitivity across socio-political and economic issues.

(l) The schools define themselves primarily in terms of creating cutting edge knowledge and hence research has become the backbone of the innovation and experimentation in these schools.

(m) The schools have evolved systems for continuous flow of feedback through alumni and corporate executives, which are disseminated, discussed and used for decision making, for research, consulting, and teaching. Unlike many Indian schools, where this is handled by placement cell, in these schools, such feedback is even taken by the Deans of the schools (for example, Deepak Jain of Kellogg School). This approach helps the schools integrate closely with the centre of action—viz. the corporate world.

(n) These schools have developed a high level of 'customerness'. There is a formal marketing cell continuously interacting with the corporate world, sensing opportunities and floating new products.

(o) Faculty development through mentoring at entry stage, liberal research funding, secondment into industry are done to develop thought and action centric faculty.

(p) In a nutshell, these B-Schools lay heavy emphasis on developing future leaders. They are characterized by experimentation, responsiveness and openness to learn, integrate with corporate world, integrate thought with action, through the type of exposure they provide and follow non-traditional pedagogies.

APPENDICES

Appendix 1a: profiles of the nine schools

An attempt is made in Appendices 1a and 1b to sketch

- the demographic profile of the students, and
- highlight the salient contours of the nine B-Schools that participated in this study.

The sample is predominantly young being 24 years and below (82.40); the rest (17.50) being older than 25 years of age. Majority (84.50) of the sample comprise males while the rest (15.50) are females. They are by and large graduates (86.60), while the rest (13.40) being either post graduates or have additional professional qualifications like CA (Chartered Accountancy).

Majority of the sample comprises those who have spent their early years in the city (71.80), followed in small numbers by those from towns (26.10) and villages (2.20). Predominantly, the students come from middle-income families (84.50), some from high-income families (12.20) and the rest (3.30) from low-income backgrounds. The father is generally a government employee (33.80), a businessman (10.60), a corporate executive (14.10) or a professional (13). The mother is typically a homemaker (67.10); some are academicians (15.10), while the rest (19) are involved in other kinds of work. Majority of the graduates (77.90) hail from nuclear families, while a minority (22.10) are from joint families. They are either the eldest (45.20) or the youngest (37.10) in the family. Very few are either the only child (6.10) or middle born (9.60); this is probably a reflection of the changing family size in urban middle class, educated India. They are predominantly influenced by a family member (72.40), followed by a public figure (13 per cent), friend (8.9) or teacher (4.9).

The family background being middle income, belonging to nuclear family with an urban upbringing, would imply high focus on academics, emphasis and reward for academic excellence at school and college levels, many times at the cost of extra-curricular activities and sports. Since they are from nuclear families, they do not get adequate scope to develop their inter-personal skills, tolerance, pro-social behaviour, and group-working orientation unless they involve themselves with extracurricular activities.

Appendix 1b: profile sketches of the nine schools

JBIMS (Jamnalal Bajaj institute of management studies)

Bajaj Institute is a department of the University of Bombay. It is one of the older schools having been established in 1965. The school building was gifted by the Bajaj family, hence the name of the school. In the late 1960s, when the UGC selected three centres of excellence in management, Bajaj was one of them, the other two being FMS-Delhi and UBS-Chandigarh.

Thus the school has been one of the leading B-Schools in India. Bajaj runs the following programmes:

- MBA—financial management,
- MBA—Marketing, MBA-HRM,
- Masters in Management Studies,
- Three year part-time evening programme in Management Studies and
- PhD in Management.

It has the following centres of excellence—ETA Learning Centre, Dubai, Personality Lab-Mumbai, Business Consulting Lab, Mumbai. Given the volume of work being done by the school, it is surprising to note that their fulltime faculty strength is not even a dozen. Their educational model seems to rely heavily on teaching support from the corporate world. Thus, teaching is done more by industry than by academia. This has helped to build in the action orientation among the graduates making them more grounded.

However, on the flip side, the school is not known for knowledge creation and one wonders how much of thought centric orientation is integrated with the action orientation in the school.

Bajaj has had a head start over schools like IIMB, IIML, MDI and NITIE. It also enjoys a tremendous locational advantage. Despite this, the school does not feature among the top five Indian schools in the annual rankings. Perhaps its greatest disadvantage is that it is part of the university system, which relatively speaking, constrains its functional autonomy unlike the other top schools in India. Owing to its small faculty size, the school has made no mark in the area of knowledge creation.

Over the years the school has built a good brand equity and track record of placements and is in a position to attract bright minds. The school has close linkage with the corporate world.

The major challenge for the school is to move from preponderant teaching mode to knowledge creation and consulting; and to also provide an appropriate blend of thought and action to the graduates of the school.

IIM-Ahmedabad (IIMA)

Indian Institute of Management, Ahmedabad was established in 1961 as an autonomous body with the active collaboration of the Government of India, Government of Gujarat, and industry. In the initial years the school had collaboration with Harvard Business School. The vision of the school from inception has been to be a fully-integrated management school with equal focus on creation, dissemination and application of knowledge through research, teaching and consulting. It is thus a truly holistic business school. It provides educational facilities for training young men and women for careers in management and related fields in different kinds of organizations. It strives to heighten the managerial skills and competencies of the practicing executives from the corporate world and administrators from other sectors. IIMA has another laudable goal (like the ITP of Harvard and ICEM of Stanford) to develop teachers and researchers in different fields of management. IIMA has established a strong reputation in the areas of graduate education, management development, research, consulting and upgrading skills of management educators.

It has the following Centres of Excellence:

- Centre for E-Governance
- Centre for Telecom Policy Studies
- National Information Centre on Management
- Infrastructure Development Centre
- Indian Public Sector in Transition
- Centre for Innovation, Incubation and Entrepreneurship
- Indian Public Sector in Transition
- Centre for Management of Health Services
- Mental Health Support Program
- Centre for Management in Agriculture Communications
- Ravi J. Matthai Centre for Educational Innovation

From the inception the school has had global orientation, global benchmarks and desire to be a global school, owing perhaps to its Harvard lineage.

This also helped the school become well known among the leading global B-Schools. Faculty from IIMA also got the opportunity to study and teach in leading schools like Harvard, Wharton, and Stanford etc. IIMA offers the following long-term programmes:

- The two years PGDBM (with an intake of 240),
- One year Executive PGDM,
- Two years programme in Agri-business, and
- Two years programme in Public Policy.

The MDPs of IIMA are highly rated and attended by senior government officials as well as senior corporate executives. IIMA has around 86 faculty trained in different B-Schools from around the world. The Fellow Programme (PhD) of IIMA is well known. In fact today, many top B-Schools have IIMA FPM alumni on their rolls. The school has the distinction of being consistently ranked number one in the annual Indian B-Schools ranking. It is also the only Indian school which featured in the top 100 global B-School rankings. IIMA has established tremendous brand equity over the years and therefore is in a position to attract the mighty talent of the country.

IIMA has got the distinction of grooming the largest number of CEOs in this country IIMA publishes a powerful journal Vikalpa modeled on the *Harvard Business Review*. This journal has established its own reputation and is well regarded for its scholarly contribution among the Indian management journals. Indian Institute of Management-Ahmedabad has been a pioneer in raising funds from the corporate world through endowments in the form of Chairs and funds for buildings.

The schools subscribes to case method as the dominant pedagogy, which tremendously helps in improving problem-solving skills. Every student in IIMA gets to study approximately 600 cases chosen from around the world.

The case-based pedagogy no doubt sharpens the analytical ability as well as decision-making capability. It however does not adequately focus on development of the total person including Emotional, Spiritual, Ethical, Aesthetic aspects, which contribute to holistic personality development.

Thus the greater challenge of IIMA is to move from the preponderant cognitive centric pedagogy to the experiential pedagogy.

IIM-Bangalore (IIMB)

IIMB was established in 1973 with a focus on grooming managerial talent for public sector organizations, which were then considered to occupy the 'commanding heights' of the economy. Ironically however, the students mostly gravitated to lucrative private jobs with few joining the public sector, the very reason behind setting up IIMB. The school also cherished the vision of being a pioneer in sectors like health, transport, education; urban planning etc., which unfortunately, did not take root. Till 1990, IIMB was preponderantly in the graduate programme with little focus on research, consulting and MDP. It was in the 1990s that the school moved from preponderant teaching focus to research, consulting, and continuing education. Thus in a sense, it adopted the IIMA model and developed itself into a fully-integrated Management School. The school has a faculty strength of ninety two, the largest faculty size in the country.

IIMB offers the two-year PGDM with an intake of 240 and a three years executive PGDM in IT and Software Management. It has been the first school in India identified for the two-year Public Policy programme by the Government of India, which is run in collaboration with the Maxwell School of Public Policy, University of Syracuse, USA. The school acquired a place of prominence in the 1990s and had built many centres of excellence. Currently, it has the following centres of excellence:

1. NSRCEL (the N.S. Raghavan Centre for Entrepreneurial Learning)

2. Software Management
3. Public Policy
4. CIRE (Centre for Insurance Research)
5. ERP (Enterprise Resource Planning)
6. CDOCTA (Centre for Case Development and Teaching Aids)
7. Corporate Governance
8. CCMR (Centre for Financial Markets and Institutions)
9. SCMC

IIMB publishes a journal, management review which has the largest circulation (among Indian B-School Journals). IIMB established a tremendous reputation for itself and many companies like donated Chairs, some of them being:

1. UTI Chair in Capital Market
2. Surrendra Paul Memorial Chair in Systems
3. Wipro Chair in Management
4. Ratan Tata Chair on Civil Society and Globalization
5. RBI Chair in Infrastructure management
6. Jamuna Ragahvan Chair in Entrepreneurship

IIMBangalore has powerful international linkages and was the first Indian school to join the league of McGill, INSEAD, University of Lancaster, International University, Tokyo, for its programme IMPM (The International Masters Program in Practicing Management).

IIMB is generally ranked among the top three schools of the country ranging from 1 to 3. IIMB has dreams of going global. It initially plans to establish a centre in Singapore. Although the school started with a public sector focus, it has today become a full fledged B-School with focus on research, consulting, continuing education, and teaching.

IIMB uses an eclectic pedagogy—case methodology, lectures, and simulations. Because of its pedagogical orientation, it powerfully inculcates broad-based intellectual orientation, exposure to business landscape along with heightening analytical and problem-solving skills. However, IIMB does not adequately focus on holistic development of the students. In this school also (as in IIMA), the focus is limited to developing managerial capabilities. In the whole process, focus on building leaders gets a backseat.

IIM-Calcutta (IIMC)

IIMC has been the first school to be established by the Government of India in 1961. Sloan School of Management-MIT was the partner school in the initial phase. The impact of MIT is very much evident in the quant-centric focus of the school. Today, IIMC is acknowledged as a leader in the field of quantitative methods and operations research.

The thrust of the school has been preponderantly teaching and therefore it could not make enough mark in consulting and continuing education, unlike MDI, IIMA and IIMB. Even today, the preponderant focus of the school is on teaching. IIMC offers two years of PGDM and two year programme in IT and Computer applications. IIMC offers a fellow programme in management. The faculty strength is 70.

Although IIMC has been the oldest school, with the MIT DNA, somehow it has never been ranked as the number one school in the country. In fact, it's ranking ranges from two to four across most annual national ranking exercises. IIMC has established four centres of excellence in management:

1. Centre for Human values,
2. Centre for Environmental Management,
3. Centre for Entrepreneurship and Innovation and
4. Centre for Corporate Governance

Over the years, the institute has established its reputation with a distinctive bias towards Quantitative Techniques. The pedagogy and faculty orientation is therefore towards analytical, statistical, and logical approach to management education.

Like IIMA and IIMB, it has also got robust international placements, which tremendously enhances its reputation and brand value for graduate programmes.

The greatest challenge for this school is to move towards becoming a fully integrated holistic school focusing equally on creation, dissemination, and application of knowledge through research, consulting, teaching, and continuing education.

The other pedagogical approaches—experiential, simulation centric, outbound theatre—are inadequately emphasized in this school. Even the case method does not get adequate emphasis as in IIMA and IIMB. Owing to this orientation, IIMC graduates are highly developed on analytical and logical capabilities. This dominant approach however does not help in holistic development of individual capabilities.

IIM-Lucknow (IIML)

IIM-Lucknow was set up as the fourth institution in the IIM chain, by the Government of India in 1985. Although it has been part of the elite IIM group, yet, for a long time it did not have the lustre of a top school, having never featured at the same level as the IIMA, IIMB, and IIMC.

In the initial phase, many of the faculty who joined the school were non PhD's, a major departure from the practice prevalent in IIMA, IIMB, and IIMC. Secondly, it is interesting that no professors of leading schools like IIMA, IIMB, and IIMC, XLRI, FMS moved to this school in the initial stages. For a long period of time, the school could not develop a scholarly temper and continued to be primarily a teaching-centric institution. Faculty size lingered around 25 for a long period. The institute had neither a PhD programme nor a journal of its own, both being the main drivers for promoting scholarly fervour.

Around 1999, the school shifted gears and moved from the preponderant teaching orientation to a fully integrated business school, focusing equally on creation, dissemination, and application of knowledge through research, teaching, consulting and continuing education. In 2001, the school launched its PhD programme and also its own journal. There was a steep increase in the faculty size from approximately 30 to 66. Consulting and research began to flourish in the school. In the period when the school tremendously expanded its consulting and training activities, it also decided to build a satellite campus in Noida, thus establishing a presence in the national capital region, and overcoming its locational disadvantage.

The school also developed the vision of becoming a global school and to this end signed nineteen MOU's across the world. In 2003, the school reached a pinnacle having been ranked number one among Indian B-Schools by Business World.

IIM-Lucknow offers the following programmes:

1. Post Graduate Program in Management,
2. PGP—Agribusiness,

3. Part time executive PGPM and
4. Fellow Program in Management

It has the following centres of excellence:

1. Innovation and Incubation Centre,
2. Agriculture Management Centre,
3. Centre for Study of Leadership and Human Values, and
4. Internet Commerce and Research Centre.

The current faculty size is 36. IIM Lucknow has excellent brand equity and its placement scenario has been very good.

MDI-Gurgaon

Management Development Institute-Gurgaon, was established as a school for continuing education in 1973 by the Industrial Finance Corporation of India (IFCI) as an autonomous body. A grant from the German institution Kreditanstalt für Wiederaufbau (KfW), routed through the IFCI, helped to set up the school. The initial objective for setting up this school was to groom and develop leaders in the financial sector. It was modeled on the Administrative Staff College of India (ASCI), Hyderabad and the dream of the school was to be the ASCI of north India. However, the school could not actualize this dream and continued to be a small and limping institution until 1985.

In 1985, the Late Shri. Rajiv Gandhi, and P. Chidambaram, then Union Minister of State, Personnel, Public Grievances and Pensions, identified MDI as a centre, to bring executives from public, private, and government sectors and groom them to be leaders for all the three sectors. To achieve this, the National Management Program

(NMP) was floated. The core objective of this fifteen months programme was to develop appreciative mindsets about the nuances and uniqueness across the three sectors among the graduates, and in turn provide opportunity to learn from each other. No doubt, MDI got a timely boost through this programme; however, it went into limbo for another long spell of seven to eight years.

In 1994, MDI decided to start the graduate PGDBM programme and in 1995, decided to be a holistic management school equally emphasizing research, continuing education, teaching and consulting. Thus, MDI is a truly integrated business school. Today, it occupies a prominent place in the B-School firmament being in the league of the top five schools of the country. Its ranking has been ranging from two to five and has, in some surveys, been ranked higher than IIML and IIMC. This is quite an achievement considering that the school has been in post graduate business education only for the last 12 years.

It is the largest school in India in the area of continuing education being far ahead of all other B-Schools. MDI today has a large faculty size i.e. 86, next only to IIMB. It runs the following programmes:

1. Two year PGPM,
2. Two year PGPM-HR,
3. Two year PGPIM—International Management,
4. Fifteen months Executive PGDBM,
5. Fifteen months Executive PGDM in Energy Management,
6. Three-year part time Executive PGPM. MDI is known for its fellowProgramme where the intake is 25 every year.

MDI has the following centres of excellence:

1. Centre for Supply Chain Management,
2. Centre for Excellence in Information Management
3. Centre for Entrepreneurship,
4. Centre for Corporate Governance,
5. Centre for Energy Management,
6. Centre for Transformational Leadership.

MDI's approach to imparting education has been truly eclectic, combining various pedagogies ranging across case method, experiential, simulation, lecture, outbound, project based, and theatre. Given its locational advantage, the school provides tremendous opportunity for students to do live industry projects.

MDI's vision has been to create thought leaders and change masters for the globe. Its vision is to be a truly global school and it has the largest number of global linkages (39) with schools in different parts of the world. MDI sends around 75–80 students on exchange and receives the same number from across the globe every year. In a nutshell, it's the fastest growing B-School, throbbing with many exciting activities (entrepreneurship, theatre, outbound, gaming, and a myriad other clubs) making this very much a happening place.

SPJIMR: S. P. Jain institute of management & research

S. P. Jain Institute of Management and Research (SPJIMR) is one of the leading B-Schools in India, ranked somewhere between seven and ten in the annual rankings. It was established through a generous grant by the Shanti Prasad Jain family and was inaugurated by Margaret Thatcher in 1981. In recent years, the school has embarked on a thrust towards becoming a global school by establishing centres outside India, Dubai and Singapore. Although it was established much later than IIMA, IIMB, IIMC, Jamnalal Bajaj, and XLRI, it has successfully built good brand equity and hence attracts good talent from different parts of the country. The placement record of this school has been quite good.

S. P.Jain offers the following academic programmes:

- PGP in Management,
- PGP in IT, PGP in family managed businesses,
- Masters Programme in IT,
- Three year part-time evening programme for practicing managers and a PhD programme.

It has the following centres of excellence:

- Centre for Project Management, E-MBA Centre,
- Centre for development of Corporate Citizenship,
- Centre for Family Managed Businesses,
- Centre for Entrepreneurship, and
- Centre for Executive Education.

This school, like other Bombay based schools relies heavily on teaching inputs from industry. This has enabled S. P. Jain to inculcate pragmatic orientation among the students. Academic thrust and knowledge creation appear to be secondary in this school and it has not yet established itself as a centre for knowledge creation, although it does have an FPM programme. It has a faculty strength of 37.

The pedagogy is eclectic, using lectures, cases and simulations. Students also do a social project in addition to the summer project (a common feature in the other top schools) to sensitize them to social issues and conditions. However, alternate pedagogies-experiential, outbound, theatre, gaming etc., which help develop the total person are not adequately emphasized.

XLRI-Jamshedpur

The Xavier Labour Relations Institute (XLRI) was set up in India as early as 1949 in Jamshedpur. It was born out of the vision of a Jesuit, Father Quinn Enright. Since then, the Jamshedpur Jesuit Society has nurtured the growth of XLRI, in keeping with its commitment to MAGIS—excellence in everything.

XLRI has two streams of regular post graduates programmes—one in Business Management and one in Personnel Management and Industrial Relations. They offer an evening three-year part time programme for working executives, an executive PG programme in distance e-learning mode and an FPM. The school has five centres of excellence:

- Centre for Human Resource Development,
- Centre for Logistics and Transport Management,
- Centre for Small Enterprises,
- Centre for Educational Management, and
- Centre for Educational Management, Leadership, and Research.

The school has a faculty strength of 40 and a batch intake of 120 in each of the full-time post graduate programmes. In line with its global aspirations, the school set up a centre in Dubai, offering a post graduate programme there since 2001.

The school uses an eclectic mix of pedagogies including lecture, cases, and simulations. Other teaching modes are not widely used. The school has a strong alumni base, excellent brand equity which helps it to attract bright talent selected by using the Xavier Admission Test (XAT). The school has excellent placements which in turn reinforces its brand equity.

XIM-Bhubaneshwar (XIMB)

The Xavier Institute of Management, Bhubhaneshwar belongs to the Xavier group of educational institutions. It was established in 1987. The founding director of the school Father De Souza, former director XLRI, moved there with four-five faculty members to start the school. The philosophy, vision, mission, and pedagogy of this school closely resemble that of XLRI. The Orissa government generously offered land and other resources to develop the infrastructure and hence this school admits a percentage of students from that state. XIMB is a fairly good school and over the years, its ranking has been around ten, ranging between nine and twelve. XIMB, like other schools in remote locations, has the problem of attracting and retaining faculty. Despite this locational disadvantage, the school has consistently maintained a faculty strength of approximately thirty two. This school has focused (like XLRI, Jamshedpur), on developing a fully-integrated management school with adequate blend of research, consulting and MDP teaching. XIMB has a decent fellow programme, thereby contributing to the development of scholars and teachers. It has developed one centre of excellence—CENDRET—Electricity Utility Research Centre. The school has done enormous work in the area of rural development, community involvement and power reforms especially in Orissa.

The student intake in the regular PG programme is 120. It also has a part-time evening PG programme for practicing managers. XIMB has a good track record of placements and the corporate world views it as one of the good schools. Overall, XIMB is a growing school, with the right kind of growth strategies built on a sound activity mix.

Perusing the brief sketches of the nine management schools in this study, one can draw the following conclusions:

1. All the nine are leading B-Schools in India.
2. Each of them has an excellent placement record.
3. They are good brands and therefore attract top talent.
4. Most of them are reasonably integrated with the corporate world.
5. Many of these schools have a vision to be global and they have international links in some form.
6. Few of the top schools notably MDI, IIMA, and IIMB are however, fully integrated focusing equally on teaching, research, and consulting. This is a desirable model for other schools to emulate, since it enables continuous development of the faculty, contribution to the corporate world through consulting and integration of new knowledge with action.
7. Most of the schools preponderantly focus on sharpening like analytical and problem-solving capabilities. Their methodology of imparting education is predominantly lecture and case based.
8. Indian B-Schools should focus equally on developing the total person—emotional, spiritual, etc. It must enable value clarification among the students, enhance their self awareness and self knowledge which can aid them to make informed choices in life.

9. Many of the schools appear to have severe problems in retention of good faculty.

10. Some of the schools are clearly in the league of some of the top global schools in terms of teaching capabilities. They are, however, far behind when it comes to the top global schools in the area of knowledge creation and consulting capability.

11. The strength of a school in terms of its capability to influence the corporate world and build sustainable competitive edge in the long run depends on its capability to do research and create cutting edge knowledge. Unfortunately, this is a serious lacuna in most of these schools. This should be the primary concern and future direction of development for these schools.

12. Indian schools should shift their undue focus from placements and salaries, to quality and quantum of contribution in the area of knowledge creation, dissemination and application and become a powerful agent of change in organizations and society.

13. Schools should also seek to develop talent with relevant competencies for the corporate world, by aligning their curriculum to stakeholder requirements.

14. Since change is happening in every field of human endeavour, schools should seek to have more frequent revamp of their curricula. Without this approach, schools will be producing graduates who need to unlearn what the schools have taught them, since it is outdated and therefore irrelevant. In fact, curricula need to be built with clarity on outcome competencies being developed.

15. Schools should establish close feedback loops to understand the changing trends in the industry and modify/change their offerings accordingly.

16. Schools should encourage the development of open cultures conducive to experimentation and innovation so that faculty can develop cutting edge curricula. Greater exposure to industry, frequent interactions and mutual learning are required.

NOTES

1. Mental structures, frameworks, assumptions and worldview.
2. Although the term androgogy (referring to adult learning) is the appropriate term, we use pedagogy since it is widely used and understood.

Index

About the Author

Asha Bhandarker is Raman Munjal Chair Professor of Leadership Studies at Management Development Institute, Gurgaon. She is a distinguished psychologist and management thinker. She was recently awarded the best teacher award 2006–08 by the students of the PGP-HR programme at MDI. She has published four books and many articles in various national and international journals. Dr Bhandarker has been a Senior Fulbrighter and has been a Visiting Professor at Darden School of Business, University of Virginia and at George Mason University (2004–2005). She has been a visiting fellow at the London Business School (1990).

RESEARCH GROUP

R Ravi Kumar is a tenured Professor in Organizational Behaviour at the Indian Institute of Management—Bangalore and is a reputed Non-Clinical Corporate Counsellor. He holds a Masters degree in Psychology and Parapsychology and a doctoral degree in Organizational Behaviour, both from Andhra University, Waltair, India. In the past Professor Kumar has been associated with the Andhra University, Osmania University, Berhampur University and Government of India's National Institute of Small Industry Extension Training that has been recognized as a centre of excellence by UNIDO for its pioneering endeavours in the area of Entrepreneurship and Small Enterprise Management.

SG Bhargava is Professor of Organizational Behaviour and Human Resource Management at the Shailesh J Mehta School of Management, IIT, Bombay. He has also taught at the Indian Institute of Management, Lucknow and Ahmedabad. He is the first recipient of the prestigious VKRV Rao Award (2003) in Management by the ICSSR, New Delhi. He is also the recipient of the ISCA Young Scientist (1986) as well as MPCOST Young Scientist (1988) awards. He is currently teaching Organizational Behaviour, Human Resource Management, Entrepreneurship Development, Buyer Behaviour, and Research Methods in Management to the MBA and Doctoral students.

Pankaj Kumar is faculty in Human Resource Management at the Indian Institute of Management—Lucknow. He has a PhD in Organizational Psychology from the University of Delhi and has extensive teaching, research, consulting, and training experience in Human Resource Management, Organizational Culture and

Effectiveness, Team Building and associated fields. He has also published several articles and presented papers in national and international conferences and seminars. He has worked on a number of consulting and research projects of USAID, NORAD, DANIDA, World Bank, AICTE and many other prestigious organizations.